Murdered Innocence

Emily Lovato

Published by Trellis Publishing, 2021.

MURDERED INNOCENCE

First edition. July 5, 2021.

Copyright © 2021 Emily Lovato.

ISBN: 979-8224463138

Written by Emily Lovato.

MURDERED INNOCENCE

EMILY LOVATO

MICHELE AVILA

Michele Yvette Avila, known as Missy to her friends and family, was born in Los Angeles California in 1968. She grew up 20 miles north of L.A. in Arleta with her mother Irene and three brothers; Ernie, Mark, and Chris. She was the focus of two books, a movie starring Patty Duke as her mother, and several TV shows. However, it was not her life that was remarkable but rather her death. At the tender age of 17, just as her life was beginning, she was murdered.

As horrible as any murder is, this one was made more heinous by the fact that Missy was murdered by those she trusted most, her best friends. The same girls whom she had grown up with on their quiet street in Arleta. Girls she had trusted implicitly with her deepest secrets. That is why the story of Missy's murder must start years before it happens when she was just eight years old when the new girl moved with her family into the house right around the corner from her own.

Karen Severson was that new girl and Missy was the first to befriend her.

Shy, awkward Karen moved into the house right around the corner from the Avila house. Missy invited Karen to her home to play dolls and the two became fast friends. They could often be seen walking arm-in-arm to school or jumping rope and sharing secrets under the willow tree in the Avila front yard.

"Then at 11:30 I went to my friends house. We played barbies, then we went swimming. After we had gone swimming, we played barbies again. Then we went swimming for a long time. (My friends name is Karen.)" This quote from Missy's diary on August 31, 1978 is typical of the other entries surrounding it. In fact, throughout the pages shared by Shavaun Avila, Missy's sister-in-law, Karen is mentioned in the same way on all but one page.

While Laura Doyle had been Missy's friend since long before Karen moved in, she was never as close to Missy as Karen had become. Karen often involved herself in anything Missy and Laura were doing. She seemed jealous of the friendship.

In junior high, both girls fell in with a drinking, drugging crowd of kids. Mark Avila, one of Missy's brothers, was quoted by the Los Angeles Times as saying, "She fell in with a bad crowd. She had to have low self-esteem to hang around with people like that."

By the time Missy and Karen reached 10th grade, events had begun to divide them. While Missy blossomed into a green-eyed beauty, Karen gained weight and began her long relationship with the green-eyed monster. It was that very jealousy which led to the sundering of the friendship and eventually to Missy's death.

Karen craved the attention Missy received. More than one person was quoted saying Karen was obsessed with Missy and wanted to be her. However, Missy was the complete opposite of Karen. Missy was outgoing, popular, and pretty. Karen was overweight, shy, and would have been completely unknown to fellow students if not for Missy. This just made Karen angrier. She blamed Missy for her lack of popularity and began trying to sabotage Missy's.

In one incident, Missy was beaten up by a group of girls who believed a rumor that she had slept with their boyfriends. One of the girls told Missy shortly after the attack that it had been Karen who started the rumor. Still fiercely loyal to her friend, Missy refused to believe that Karen would do that. "Missy was so mad at the girl for telling her it was Karen's fault. Missy 'knew' Karen would never do anything like that." Irene Avila would later say. "Missy made great lasagna, dreamed of becoming a physical therapist, and was fiercely loyal to her childhood friends."

In her junior year, Missy dated a boy named Randy. After a month, she broke up with him because he liked to drink and do drugs too much. He soon started dating Karen and they moved into an apartment together. This soon became party central despite the fact that Karen had given birth to a baby girl she named Stephanie after her sister and that infant was present. Missy told her mother of an incident where Randy pulled her onto his lap just as Karen walked in. Missy quickly got up and told Randy she wasn't interested in dating him again. She suggested Karen leave him. "Karen was really upset because the guy she wanted didn't want her," recalls Irene. "He wanted Missy."

In a similar incident, Laura Doyle's boyfriend, Victor Amaya, had broken up with her due to her constant jealousy. "I broke off the relationship because she was jealous of me talking to other girls, including Missy. Laura refused to accept the breakup and became bitter." Victor would later say.

One day, Laura's drives by Victor's while he and Missy are holding hands and kissing at the end of his driveway. Enraged, she pulls down her window to tell them that they were caught and call Missy names like 'slut' and 'whore.' Instead of apologizing and denying any feelings for Missy as Laura had expected him to, Victor tells her to go away. "We (he and Missy) argued with Laura at my house in Arleta. Me, my brother Noah and Missy had been standing in front of the house when Laura drove up. Laura wanted to know 'Why is Missy here?' and I ordered Laura to leave. Before she drove away she said 'I'm going to kill that bitch!' I didn't take the threat seriously and I never reported it to police."

By September 1985, both Karen and Laura had stopped speaking to Missy. She was divested by the loss of her two closest friends. On September 21st, Karen sees Missy at a local park and attacks her with a beer bottle. She slaps and pushes her former confidant before friends break up the fight. Missy's mother heard of the confrontation but did not later connect it to her daughter's murder. After all, the girls had often quarreled during their long friendship.

"Her only problem, at least on that fateful day was that she was very popular with the boys and this drove Laura Doyle and Karen Severson crazy." Deputy District Attorney Tamia Hope said at the trial. "They started out yelling at her, telling her how mad they were at her, and how she slept with entirely too many boys and messed up entirely too many relationships."

Shortly after that confrontation, the girls apologize to Missy and make up. According to her mother, her excitement was easily noticeable. She is thrilled to have her two best friends back in her life.

On October 2nd, Missy told her mother she was going out with Laura. "When Laura got to the house, the girls were laughing and talking about boys. As they drove off they seemed very carefree. I remember how especially pretty Missy looked that day. She was all excited to go. She even turned to me and said "I love you" which is something she did not ordinarily do. That scene haunts me even today."

They met up with Karen and her roommate Eva Chirumbolo at Stonehurst Park in Sun Valley. From there they drove in two separate cars to Wicky up, also known as Colby Canyon. A spot all three girls were familiar with as it was a popular party spot for teens. A campground in the Angeles State Forest a 45 minute drive from Arleta.

"Karen said that she and Laura 'planned to scare Avila.' I didn't know what they had planned. I didn't know how far this was going to go." Eva would later say at Laura and Karen's trail.

What happened next is pieced together by the three girls testimony. When they reach the forest, they park in a dirt lot near a wooded area near the creek. Laura and Karen get out of their vehicles and begin yelling at Missy who is still sitting in Laura's car. Missy begins crying and the girls force her out of the car and begin pushing her around calling her names and accusing her of stealing their boyfriends.

Eva says she decided to get out of the vehicle as by this point the confrontation was becoming increasingly intense. Missy, who had just been laughing and listening to music with who she believed were her best friends was not crying and noticeably shaking with fear. Laura grabs her wrist and forcibly pulls her towards a trail into the wooded area. Missy resists until Karen comes up and pushes her.

"All four of us walked down an embankment to the creek. Laura and Karen continued screaming at Missy," says Eva, the prosecution's star witness. She continues her retelling of that fateful night's events by saying Laura yanks Missy by her hair and accuses her of sleeping with Victor. She steps up to the creek and pushes Missy towards Karen who shoves her to the ground.

Missy is frantic and begs for forgiveness and frantically pleads for her life. At this point, Eva says she became terrified of what was to come and runs back to the car. "I was scared so I ran back to where the cars were parked," says Eva. She hears Missy scream for her to help her but she feels helpless and feared for her own life. Unlike the obese Karen and aggressive Laura, both Missy and Eva are petite and no physical match for either girl let alone both of them at once.

Karen and Laura continue to beat and batter Missy. One of her earrings is ripped from her ear and becomes tangled in her hair. Her beautiful waist length hair is hacked at with some sharp instrument and clumps of it litter the ground. Laura shouts, "You're going to pay for what you've done! You're going to pay for sleeping with our boyfriends!"

They carry the 98 pound Missy, as she struggled to escape, down to the shallow water, a mere 8 inches deep. As she continues to struggle they forcefully hold her head under the water. They continued to hold her head underwater for several minutes after she quit struggling and then carry a 4-foot, 100 pound log over and put it on her neck to keep her head under the water.

Still scared, Eva asked Laura several times, "What happened? Where's Missy?" She was told that she was drowned. She testified that while both Laura and Karen appeared jittery after the murder but they weren't sorry they had done it. "A few minutes later, Karen and Laura joined me. Karen Severson jumped into her car and drove away. When I got into the car with Laura, she said 'We killed Missy.' Then she said, 'Missy deserved to die because she slept with Victor.'"

Four hours after the murder, Laura called the Avila house and asked to speak with Missy. Irene was confused. "I told her I thought Missy was with her," she says. Laura informed her that she'd dropped Missy off to talk with three boys in a blue Camaro while she went to get gas. When she came back, Missy and the boys were gone.

Three days later, on October 5th, hikers found Missy's body right where the girls had left her, face down in the creek with a log anchoring her in the water. One of the first policemen on the scene said, "The young woman's body was a terrifying sight." Her face was badly beaten and her hair was chopped off.

When the police came to inform Irene Avila that they had found Missy, she collapsed. At the funeral, she collapsed again and had to be rushed to the hospital by ambulance. The grisly murder of her only daughter was simply too much for Irene to bear. Both Karen and Laura attended the funeral of their 'best friend.' Eva Chirumbolo did not.

Shortly after the funeral, Karen and her 2-year-old daughter moved in with Irene. Karen vowed to find the 'animal' that murdered her friend and 'helped' Irene track down clues. She lived with Irene for three months sitting up nights sharing memories of Missy. Irene Avila said, "She was close to me, like another daughter. Karen was my daughter's best friend. They grew up together."

Karen was obsessed with the murder. She visited Missy's grave two or three times a week, often leaving balloons or flowers. The walls of her bedroom with pictures of her dead friend and newspaper articles about her murder. Worse, she began frequently visiting the scene of the murder and was seen sitting by the creek drinking beer.

The cover up began falling apart when Karen announced out of the blue that Laura wanted to change her story. Karen then summoned Laura to Irene's house where she told Missy's mother that she had lied. There was never any blue Camaro or any boys. She now claimed that the truth was she had dropped Missy off near a L.A. church to deliver $500 to a drug dealer.

Not long after that Karen claimed that Missy was haunting her. She claimed to see her sitting on the Avila's couch, floating over her while she slept, and even keeping her car from starting while visiting Missy's grave.

The mystery of who murdered Missy Avila might have never been solved if it weren't for the suicide of Eva Chirumbolo's brother which made her understand the loss the Avila family felt. She finally came forward in July of 1988 and told police everything. She was not charged as an accessory to murder in exchange for her full cooperation.

Based on her recounting of the events, Karen Severson and Laura Doyle were arrested and charged with 1st degree murder. Their trial date was set for September 18, 1989. Both women plead 'not guilty' and Karen told officers, "I know the details of what happened to Missy but I'm not going to say."

Irene's grief is worsened by the shock of having intimately shared it with the woman who caused it. "She was Missy's best friend," says Irene, "but she was jealous of Missy's family, Missy's looks, Missy's popularity and even Missy's relationship with me." Missy's brother Mark, 24, agrees. "Karen, wanted to be Missy," he said to People.

Yet if Karen had been full of love and hate, jealousy and guilt, she kept it hidden. "We talked to Karen several times during the investigation," says L.A. Deputy Sheriff Bill Patterson, "and not once—I mean never—did we suspect she was in on the murder."

"When they told me that it was Karen and Laura, I didn't believe the cops," Avila said. "I couldn't believe it. I couldn't believe it."

Irene never suspected Karen either, it was beyond her comprehension that someone so close to Missy could have been involved in the killing. "Who knows, maybe Missy was haunting Karen to make her pay for what she did," says Irene. "If it's possible, then I hope to God she's haunting her each night in prison."

On January 31, 1990 both Laura Doyle and Karen Severson, both now 22, were convicted of 2nd degree murder. The prosecutor pushed hard for a 1st degree murder conviction saying, "Our position was that this crime was a deliberate, well-planned torture and execution of Missy, and needed to be treated as such," one prosecutor told the Daily News 11 years ago, after Doyle's parole was denied. However, several jurors said afterwards that they and not been convinced that the murder was planned in advance rather than a crime of passion.

Both women received 15 years to life. Karen served her time at the California Institution for Women in Corona, California. Laura, however, was sent to Valley State Prison for Women in Chowchilla, California.

They first became eligible for parole in 1997. During parole hearings, Karen admits she arranged the walk in the woods but says she only planned to torment Missy. Laura also becomes more forthright at her parole hearings and in 2002 she admits to coaxing Missy into the water and killing her but insists that Karen was the ringleader.

During her incarceration, Karen is described as the modal inmate. She was active in self-help groups, Bible studies, tutoring fellow inmates, and earned a Bachelor of Arts degree in psychology and a doctorate in theology. She was also diagnosed with Multiple Sclerosis during her time in prison.

On July 8, 2011, the parole board recommended Karen Severson's release despite the Avila family's objections. Irene Avila was not able to attend this parole hearing for health reasons. After a 2001 parole hearing for Karen, Irene suffered a heart attack and was ordered by her doctors to never attend another one.

Karen's parole was subject to a four month board review period and then the governor has a chance to intervene. While prosecutors say their hands are tied, the Avila family held out hope and began collecting letters opposing her release to send to Governor Brown.

None of their attempts were successful however, and Karen was release on parole. Upon hearing of Severson's release, Irene Avila said, "I wish that girl would die. I feel bad for my sons. I feel bad for everybody who knew her. This was a terrible injustice, a terrible injustice. I don't understand why people who commit murder, they let 'em out." Laura Doyle was paroled shortly after Karen Severson.

The wounds of loss were ripped wide open with the release of Missy's murders. "I hate her. I hate her. I hate her," said Irene Avila, now 72 upon hearing of Laura Doyle's release. "Both should have suffered the death penalty. They are free. My daughter is in the ground."

One would think the story ends there, but it does not.

Despite public outcry, Karen Severson wrote a memoir about the case entitled "My Life, I Lived It." In the memoir, she recounts explicit details of the murder. When asked about the memoir, Karen said, "I walked away. They don't have a daughter. They don't have a sister. I don't have a friend."

When told that there were several other ways she could make money, Karen said, "Like what, sell myself?" Severson told those who questioned the morality of her making money off of her crime that she would donate a portion of the proceeds to an anti-bullying group. When asked why she does not donate all of the proceeds, Severson responded, "I didn't say everything. I have to live. It's hard to get a job out there."

Unfortunately the 1st Amendment says criminals cannot be prevented from telling their stories. However, the Avila family filed a wrongful death civil lawsuit against Severson and the book's distributor for slander and infliction of emotional distress.

"Today we're filing a lawsuit against a vicious killer who has been profiting off her crime," Shavaun Avila, Missy's sister-in-law told news sources outside court. "It's not about us making money off this lawsuit, it's about letting the public know that crime is paying in California."

In addition to the civil lawsuit, the Avila family pushed legislation in the state assembly called "Missy's Law." It's intended to help family members of crime victims recoup money from a perpetrator who has made money from a book or movie deal based on their crime. The bill was sponsored by State Assembly member Nora Campos.

"This law should have been passed a long time ago," Irene Avila said. "It's like they're giving them a reward for killing somebody."

In response to public outcry and the pending lawsuits, the distributor of Karen Severson's book changed the price to zero, ensuring she would never profit from it.

On October 15th, 2015 Governor Jerry Brown of California passed Missy's Law. The family celebrated it as a huge victory. "I feel like we've won a really big battle, but there's still a war going on out there, and we're going to keep battling as long as it takes," said Shavaun Avila.

For her part, Irene Avila has this to say, "All I can say is, `Girls, watch out whom you trust.'"

THE MURDER OF FAITH HEDGEPETH

JESSI DAVIS

Happy-go-lucky

In 1982, Connie Hedgepeth had her hands full with two teenage daughters and a husband who was addicted to drugs. Her marriage was struggling when she took a pregnancy test, hoping the result would be negative. It wasn't. Her youngest daughter was born eight months later, and Connie named her Faith.

"I felt like it was my faith in God that helped me through that situation," she said. "My faith helped me to continue to work and to do what I needed to do for my children."

Still, Connie divorced her husband when Faith was still young. Struggling to stay afloat, Connie turned to her oldest daughter, Rolanda, for support. Despite an almost 18-year age difference, Rolanda and Faith developed a strong bond – "part mother-daughter, part sister," Rolanda explained.

"We were always close. I was kind of like a second mom, but there was that sister bond, too," she said.

Rolanda's daughter Alexis was born on Faith's first birthday, and the two girls grew up together in rural North Carolina. Her upbringing was difficult, but Faith's positive attitude and eagerness to contribute propelled her through her schooling. She was an honor student, a cheerleader, and a regular volunteer for many other clubs and organizations.

"She always had this energy about her," Rolanda recalled. "She was really happy-go-lucky."

Faith's father had dropped out of college to raise his family, and Faith intended to pick up where her dad had left off. She earned a Gates Millennium Scholarship to the University of North Carolina at Chapel Hill – the very school her father had been attending. Poised to be the very first college graduate in her family, Faith had plans to become a pediatrician or a teacher once she completed her education.

Instead, the Native American biology major never made it to her 20th birthday. Police records reveal that Faith was last seen alive at approximately 3 a.m. on September 7, 2012, when she and her roommate Karena Rosario came home after an evening partying at a local nightclub.

The Thrill of a lifetime

The night before she was murdered, Faith had been studying with Karena at the Davis Library, on the university campus. At around 8 or 8:30 p.m., Faith took a break from her studies to send a text to her father – "Hey Daddy, I love you," the message read. She also texted her niece, reminding her to register to vote in the upcoming election.

At around midnight, the girls left the library and stopped back at their apartment before heading out at approximately 1 a.m. to arrive at a nightclub called The Thrill.

Just after 2:30 a.m., the girls left the bar. Karena was feeling sick after having had too much to drink, and wanted to go home. Faith helped Karena get into bed, and then fell asleep herself. However, a text message from Faith's phone was received at 3:40 a.m. by Brandon Edwards, Karena's ex-boyfriend.

"Hey b. can you come over here please," the message read. "Karena needs you more aha. You know. Please let her know you care."

A few minutes later, another text comes through that simply says, "than." It is suspected that the message was intended to fix a typo in the original message, correcting it to say "Karena needs you more *than* you know." Brandon didn't reply until the next day, when Faith's phone received a text at 4:16 p.m. that read, "Who is this?"

At around 4:30 a.m., Karena left the apartment to go over to a friend's house – and claims that she did see Faith asleep at that time. When she returned at around 11 a.m., however, she found her roommate's body in her room, in her bed, "covered by a blanket on top of her slightly askew mattress with large amounts of blood."

At 11:01 a.m., a 911 call came from the house.

Faith was unconscious and cold, Karena told the dispatcher who took the call, and there was "blood everywhere." She said she thought there may have been an altercation, explaining to the dispatcher that "there were items in the room that were not hers and that it looked like someone else had been there."

Police responded immediately, securing the scene at the girls' apartment complex and collecting evidence. They found Faith's body "positioned on the floor, leaning against the bed, with her shirt pulled up and no clothes from the waist down."

Medical examiners concluded that the cause of death was blunt force trauma, based on the severe beating Faith had endured. When the autopsy report was unsealed nearly two years after the killing, it was revealed that she also had bruises and cuts all over her arms and legs, as well as blood underneath her fingernails.

"It's very, very hard, learning of how Faith died," said Rolanda. "She was beaten, she was bludgeoned to death. A lot of people don't understand what that means, but it was really bad."

A rape kit had also been performed, indicating the presence of semen – with DNA that matched other DNA that police had recovered at the scene. Law enforcement officials have not confirmed whether the sexual activity was consensual or forced.

Searching for suspects

In the years since Faith's death, multiple search warrants have been executed – as well as numerous court orders for things like cell phones, computers, and even social media accounts. DNA testing has also been carried out on many of men that interacted with Karena and Faith while they were at the nightclub, but so far, investigators have found no matching results.

While at The Thrill, Faith was reportedly dancing with a man named David Bell. He told police he didn't know Faith very well, and was not named by police as a suspect during the investigation.

"(Redacted) was identified as walking out of Club Thrill with Faith Hedgepeth shortly before the homicide occurred," read a police report unsealed in 2014. "He was the last male to be seen with her before her death."

The report added that Bell admitted to talking with Faith the night she was killed, and to meeting her the weekend before. He refused to provide investigators with a sample of his DNA, claiming that he had likely touched her at some point during the night of the homicide. His statements to law enforcement officers were also determined to be "inconsistent" with statements provided by others.

Another man, Jacob Beatley, was interviewed by police and also not named as a suspect. Karena visited him during the early morning hours of September 7, after leaving the apartment she shared with Faith. DNA was also sought from a man named Reginald Leonard Jackson II, who was not named as a suspect despite having been texting regularly with Faith in the days prior to her murder.

However, none of this information was offered to Faith's family until the documents were unsealed in 2014.

"All they have said to us and to the public, to the media, to everybody, (is) that this wasn't random – how do they know that?" said Chad Hedgepeth, Faith's brother. "Do they have a suspect? Do they have any suspects? ... Tell us something, because being in the dark on any and everything these past four weeks has been brutal."

While the recording from the 911 call seems to indicate that Karena was alone when she discovered Faith's body in their apartment, the police report stated that she returned to their home with a friend. In the recording, however, Karena consistently claims "I just walked into my apartment," instead of saying "we." There is also no sound recorded that could be attributed to another person in the room.

An analysis of the call could suggest that the repetition of the statement "I just walked into my apartment" is an attempt to establish an alibi – especially since the recording reveals that Karena says this several times before even providing the dispatcher with necessary information like the victim's state or the location of the emergency.

At no point in the call does Karena specifically ask for help for the victim. She also apologizes to the dispatcher, using language that analysts typically see in calls where guilty knowledge is indicated.

Initially, law enforcement turned their attention to Eriq Takoy Jones – an ex-boyfriend of Karena's who lived in the same apartment complex and was reportedly an aspiring rapper. Just a few months before the murder, Karena had filed a restraining order against Eriq, on the basis of domestic assault. Police had previously investigated claims that Eriq had kicked two of the doors in the girls' apartment completely off their frames, and eyewitness accounts reported that Karena had been seen with visible injuries to her body – inflicted, she said, by her ex-boyfriend.

"Faith took Karena to take out a restraining order," said Faith's father, Roland Hedgepeth. "I think that very possibly, Takoy may have had some ill feelings toward Faith for doing that."

Rolanda said Faith had moved in with Karena after the restraining order had been filed, to help her friend as she recovered from the abusive relationship.

"I wasn't worried about Faith at the time," Rolanda said. "I wanted them to be safe. I just wanted both of them to be safe."

Just before Faith was murdered, Eriq posted a chilling message on his Facebook page, and texted a similar message to an acquaintance.

"Deal Lord," the post read. "Forgive me for all of my sins and the sins I may commit today. Protect me from the girls who don't deserve me and the ones who wish me dead today."

An unnamed person who claimed to be a former roommate of Faith's called the Chapel Hill Police Department the day after Faith's body was discovered with additional concerning information about Eriq. According to the caller, Faith had told her that Karena's boyfriend hated her (Faith) and told her that if Karena wouldn't get back together with him, he would kill Faith.

However, Eriq was very cooperative with law enforcement during the investigation into Faith's murder. Both his apartment and car were combed for trace evidence, and his DNA was tested and cleared.

"From what I knew of her (Faith), she was the sweetest person in the world. If you needed her and she could do it, she was there," Eriq told news reporters after Faith's murder. "I'll be honest with you – whoever did this deserves to burn."

Investigators also learned that the ex-boyfriend of Karena's that Faith had texted in the hours before she was killed had also been present that night at The Thrill. Police records indicated that Brandon Edwards had even spent the night at the girls' apartment the night before the murder – making his response to Faith's texts the day she was killed quite unusual.

According to a friend named Marisol Rangel, Karena and Brandon were "just friends" at the time of Faith's murder. Marisol is the friend who was reportedly with Karena when she discovered Faith's body, but the 911 operator was confident that Karena was alone when the call was placed.

In January 2013, police released a profile of the killer. According to the profile, developed by Chapel Hill Police and the FBI's Behavioral Analysis Unit, the person responsible for Faith's murder might have been familiar with her – and possibly even lived near her in the past.

The individual may have also "made comments" about Faith in the past, with their behavior shifting after the murder occurred. Obviously, the profile indicated this person would have been "unaccounted for" during the early morning hours of September 7, 2012. Police also stated the DNA evidence collected at the scene of the homicide points toward a "male suspect."

At the time, Faith's father Roland said the development of the profile marked a "new beginning" in the investigation, and believed it would help police solve the case.

"For us, we're kind of stuck back on September 7," he said. "Every day, we get up and relive that day. But I'm confident things will open up soon."

Strange evidence

Nearly two years after the murder, police released a shocking and mysterious piece of evidence. A spiteful, handwritten note was found scrawled on a fast food bag left near the crime scene, with the words "I'M NOT STUPID BITCH JEALOUS."

Police believe the note was written by the killer, but have not said whether the handwriting has ever been officially analyzed. According to private investigator and forensic handwriting examiner Peggy Walla, some clues can be determined from the note.

"What struck me was how clean the document is – the crime scene was pretty bloody, and there's nothing on this document," she said. "Looking at it, I would get the impression it was either written outside of the crime scene, or it was written before, like a premeditation."

She also feels the words were written by a non-dominant hand, indicating that whoever wrote the note was attempting to "disguise" their penmanship. The block letters could be taken as the writer's attempt to distance themselves from authority, she said.

"The word and sentence phrase 'I'm not stupid' is a hot push-button factor," Walla added. "That's probably the most important thing said. This was a jealous person who was called 'stupid.' The person that said it who is now deceased has no way of repeating this person is stupid, which is another way to shut them up."

Users of online forums have also speculated that the use of the word 'jealous' could indicate that the writer of the note was a woman, as the word is thought to be more frequently used by females. The formation of the letter 'P' in particular has also struck some as seeming feminine in nature.

Other speculation surrounds the intent of the note. The words 'jealous' and 'bitch' suggest that the note was not meant for the police of for the public – rather, these deeply personal words were likely intended toward Faith, or possibly even Karena, who would eventually find the body. But more curious yet is the situation that must have occurred that led to the writing of the note. What happened before Faith was murdered?

Cries for help

A clue may be found in a voicemail left for a friend the night of her death. The call appears to have been a pocket-dial – a very timely pocket-dial that potentially recorded the final minutes of Faith's life. The timestamp on the nearly unintelligible message indicates that the call was made while Faith was still at The Thrill, but some have argued that a glitch in technology could have resulted in an incorrect time.

According to President and CEO of Creative Forensic Services Arlo West, who is certified by the New York Institute of Forensic Audio in enhancement, authentication, and analysis of both audio and video, the names 'Rosie' and 'Eriq' appear throughout the recording – potentially referring to Karena Rosario and her ex-boyfriend Eriq Takoy Jones.

"I've worked on hundreds, if not thousands, of cases where people have pocket-dialed somebody," West said. "If you can peel back those layers of noise, you start to get a better picture of the dialogue that is contained – stuff that starts to make a little more sense."

In his analysis for Crime Watch Daily, West identified two distinct female voices – one which he claimed is Faith Hedgepeth, and the other he describes as a "very angry female." He also picked out at least two male voices.

"I hear what I believe is Miss Hedgepeth's cries for help," West said. "You can hear her emotive voice, the tone of her voice, is clearly in pain ... You can clearly hear what I believe is Faith pleading. She's being hurt, being attacked."

West said he feels "very confident" about hearing the names 'Rosie' and 'Eriq,' and included both names in his transcript of the three-minute recording.

He also claims iPhones were "inherently problematic with timestamping" during the time Faith was killed – which he said accounts for the timestamp on the voicemail showing 1:23 a.m., while police believe Faith was killed sometime after 4:30 a.m. Still, Chapel Hill police did contact West for an official analysis of the recording.

"If it is Faith being murdered, and captured in this recording – which I think it is, this is pivotal," West said. "It should be able to solve this case."

Police seem to believe that the voicemail was recorded from the club, not from the apartment – and in the middle of the call, there appears to be music playing or someone rapping. There is also no evidence to support that the name 'Rosie' could have referred to Karena, and Eriq Takoy Jones was apparently called 'Takoy' by his friends.

Still, the voicemail is difficult to discount – especially since, on the night Faith was murdered, it appears to have recorded an emotionally-charged, angry discussion. To many listeners, including members of Faith's family, the voices sound agitated – belligerent, fast-speaking – and seem to be punctuated by audible yelps of what could be pain.

"From day one, I heard my daughter screaming in the background," said Faith's father, Roland. "I knew something was going on."

"A really good case."

The note, the voicemail audio, and other documents – including the 15-page autopsy – were unsealed in September 2014. According to Chris Blue, Chapel Hill Police Chief, the effort was an attempt to generate new leads in the investigation.

"We have excellent evidence – we have a really good case," he said. "We just need to connect this really good case with the killer."

However, in those two years, police had been unable to connect any potential suspect with the crime. The official documents were sealed during that time despite repeated requests from lawyers and news organizations to open them to the public, as investigators felt releasing the information would compromise their efforts.

"It's not that it might hinder this investigation, it will hinder this investigation," said Durham County Assistant District Attorney Charlene Franks.

She added that details contained within the documents, including the 911 call where the crime scene and body are vividly described, could help police identify the killer – as that information would have been known by very few people.

In a "cold case," Franks said, police will often turn to the public for assistance. However, since the investigation into Faith's murder is ongoing, solving the case means keeping the public – including Faith's family – in the dark about some vital details.

"The most important thing to them and the state and the Chapel Hill Police Department is to find the killer of their baby girl, Faith Hedgepeth," she said. "The only way to do that is to keep those items sealed because the information contained in there, other than (investigators), only the killer knows."

According to Steve Hale, private investigator and retired homicide detective who was never involved with the case, it's typical for law enforcement to keep the details of a case under wraps – interviews and tips that haven't been influenced by media reports can make or break a case.

"If there is a suspect, he may not know he's a suspect, and they're waiting for him to get careless and maybe make a comment to an accessory after the fact," he said, adding that detectives likely suspected someone who knew Faith and might have had a distinct motive.

Each document pertaining to the case was reviewed by Judge Howard Manning before being unsealed in 2014. Still, three investigators with the Chapel Hill Police Department and State Bureau of Investigation continued working exclusively on the unsolved case – and offered a reward of $40,000 for any information leading to the arrest and conviction of Faith's killer.

"We really want to bring some peace to Faith's family," said Blue. "This has been two unimaginable years for them."

"Your imagination starts to run wild."

Connie was contacted three hours after Faith's body was found, by a crisis counselor who told her little more than that her 19-year-old daughter Faith had been found dead in her apartment – the victim of what appeared to be a violent homicide.

"I said, 'you must have the wrong girl,'" Connie remembers. "She told me it was her, and I said, 'I don't think so.'"

It fell on Connie to contact the rest of the family, spreading the devastating news to her son, her ex-husband, and her eldest daughter, Rolanda. At that point, Connie said, she didn't have much to tell them other than that Faith was dead.

"They couldn't tell us very much because they didn't want to jeopardize the investigation," she explained. "Not knowing anything at all... your imagination starts to run wild."

Even after detectives brought the family to Chapel Hill, about 80 miles away from their home in Hollister, Connie still had no answers to her many questions. She wasn't even permitted to visit the crime scene, or see her youngest daughter.

"I just wanted to hold her hand, to let her know I was there," Connie recalled. "I still cry for my baby, and I wonder if she called out for help. Did she cry for me? These are the things you think."

Finally, the family was told the cause of death – but without any kind of motive or indication of what could have happened to lead up to Faith's murder, the new information was difficult for the family to process.

"It is getting harder, not knowing what happened, trying to accept what happened," said Rolanda. "She was beautiful. She didn't deserve it. She had a lot going for her."

While no arrests have been made, and no suspects even identified, Chapel Hill Police Lt. Josh Mecimore said police are still confident that the killer will be found and brought to justice.

"Someone knows something, and we're continually appealing to the public to come forward," he said. "This is not a cold case. We are still following up on things, still pounding the pavement, still waiting for that one piece of evidence that will help us solve this case."

Connie, Rolanda, and the rest of the Hedgepeth family are clinging to the same hope.

"At some point, God will let us know what happened," Rolanda said. "Even when I'm down, I still believe that we will find that person."

However, neighbours remain concerned as a result of the limited information available – and the fact that police have yet to make an arrest. While law enforcement officers continued to reassure nearby residents that the incident was an isolated event, neighbours wanted more answers.

"It's not a reassuring thought to wonder if you can send your kids to safety to the bus stop or if something could happen," said Anna Salomon, who lived with her husband and children in the subdivision next to the apartment complex where Faith was murdered. In the weeks following the killing, the neighbours banded together to walk children to the bus stop in collective groups.

Keeping Faith alive

One year after Faith was killed, students at the University of North Carolina gathered on campus at the Bell Tower Amphitheatre for a silent walk in celebration of the student's life. She was also made an honorary member of the Alpha Pi Omega Sorority, the country's oldest Native American Greek letter organization.

"She was the happiest person I knew, always laughing, always smiling," said Faith's friend Leslie Locklear.

Another friend, Victoria Chavis, remembered Faith's "bubbly personality."

"She had a smile that was just infectious," she said, "and she was a wonderful person to be around."

"The entire Carolina community grieves for the loss of this promising, vibrant student," added UNC Chancellor Carol Folt.

The family has honored Faith's memory by establishing the "Faith's Smile Scholarship" in her name – an award which will go to Native American women entering their freshman year of college. The scholarship project gives the family something positive to focus on while they continue searching for answers.

"It's really hard – hard because of not knowing what happened and not knowing why it happened, who did it," Rolanda added. "One little piece of information could break the case, could give us some type of peace. How could somebody withhold that, after everything we have lost?"

Still, for Connie, nothing can extinguish the shining light that defined her youngest daughter, Faith – no matter how many years go by with the case remaining unsolved.

"We don't want anyone to forget her smile. She was a beautiful girl, she was my baby," Connie said. "Her spirit is right here today."

THE MURDER OF IRA YARMOLENKO

On a seemingly normal Thursday afternoon on the Catawba River in May of 2008, two jet skiers planned on having a picnic together along the river when they stumbled upon a peculiar sight that would change their lives forever - a car crashed into a stump on the banks of the river along with the horrifying sight of a dead body lying next to it. They quickly alerted authorities and soon discovered that the body was that of a deceased young woman.

This was the tragic fate of Irina "Ira" Yarmolenko, a University of North Carolina college student who had just celebrated her twentieth birthday several days earlier. She was discovered with three items from her car tied around her neck. There was no sign of a struggle or any clear indication of a motive. She was not sexually assaulted or robbed.

Although first responders initially thought her death could have been a suicide, her death was ruled a homicide by asphyxiation. To this day, her murder still garners interest from the public due to the strange yet disturbing circumstances surrounding her death. Add to that the whispers that surround the case about the possibility that her convicted murderer, Mark Carver, might actually be an innocent man. What followed this horrific discovery was an investigation into the crime scene and into her personal life to uncover what happened to Ira.

Ira's early life and college experience

Ira Yarmolenko was born in the Ukraine on May 2nd, 1988 but emigrated to the United States when she was eight, along with her parents and brother Pavel. The family reportedly fled the Ukraine as refugees due to religious persecution. Her parents, both research scientists, were able to find job opportunities in North Carolina.

Ira quickly picked up the language and by all accounts seemed to assimilate well into American culture. She lived in North Carolina for most of her life, spoke with a southern accent and had several personal interests. Like most teenagers, she enjoyed hiking, acting, photography, sports, and music.

She also played the piano and liked listening to bands, such as the Counting Crows. She was also extremely academic. She excelled in math and science while being an active member of her high school poetry team. Ira was especially close to her family. Although she left Chapel Hill for UNC Charlotte, about a 3-hour drive away, she spoke to her mother almost every day. After her death, her mother said to reporters, "I don't think what I'm living is called life anymore."

During her two years in college, she found other interests beyond her required coursework at UNC Charlotte, where she was an undeclared major but had a strong interest in French. She was a photographer for the University Times, her college paper, and occasionally wrote columns and articles for the Niner Online, an online student-run newspaper.

She was also a member of the university's Russian Club as Russian was her first language. Her Russian language classmate described her as, "the kind of girl that always made you feel special, wanted, needed, cared for, and loved. It always seemed like she was always so happy to see you, and would always take at least a second of her time to say hello to you." It was here that she met her roommate Masha, another student from the Ukraine.

Masha and Ira bonded over the fact that they both spoke Russian and came from similar backgrounds. Masha described the day that she found out Ira was murdered when two investigators showed up at the small apartment that she shared with Ira, "It was her student I.D. picture. And I just started screaming. Sorry. Both of our families immigrated here to this country for a better life and sacrificed so much." Like most people close to Ira, Masha was devastated to hear the news of her friend's death.

Most people who knew Ira described her as outgoing. They felt that she would not have been afraid if a stranger had approached her. She was involved on campus and worked at a local coffee shop, Jackson's Java. Years after her death, her picture could still be found on the counter of Jackson's Java. She had a lasting impact on those that knew her. Her brother said, "Everything that she's ever done was to help people."

At UNC Charlotte, she had many close friends and acquaintances who described her as a cheerful and bubbly person, yet still high-achieving. In addition to her job at the coffee shop, Ira also worked as an aid in a computer lab on campus. The week before finals, her roommate Masha and friends threw a party for her 20th birthday.

During this party, her friends reported that Ira ended up cooking for everyone there, despite the fact that party was a celebration in her honor. This was not uncommon for her to do and was just the kind of person she was. Her friends concluded the celebration by visiting an art exhibit. They reported that she was in good spirits and that they parted amicably.

Although it seemed Ira was thriving in her environment at UNC Charlotte, she was in the process of closing her chapter there and beginning a new one at UNC-Chapel Hill, a school a bit closer to home. "Ira indicated she was sad to leave her friends behind at UNCC, but she was looking forward to attending UNC-Chapel Hill in the fall," according to Sgt. Tindall, an investigator in the case.

She had resigned from her positions at the coffee shop and in the computer lab where she had worked during her sophomore year shortly before she was murdered. Her brother Pavel, a then Ph.D. graduate student at Duke said, "She was not sure how she felt about leaving Charlotte. But she was very, very excited about coming to Chapel Hill."

Ira intended on transferring to UNC-Chapel Hill to be closer to her family and to major in public health. The day of her murder, she visited the coffee shop and said goodbye to her friends there and left a gift, a book, for her former boss. She also took several items to the Goodwill to donate and visited her credit union where she deposited some checks before heading to the river about 20 miles away.

The scene of the crime

The Catawba River is over 200 miles long and spans two states. It is located about 20 minutes from Charlotte and is popular among fisherman, boaters and jet skiers. First responders on that fateful day described a perplexing, yet disturbing scene.

The doors on the driver's side of Ira's car were opened, and her body was found just a few feet away. It did not appear she was sexually assaulted or robbed, nor did she have defensive wounds from fighting off her attacker or attackers.

Three ligatures were found around her neck: a nylon ribbon from a bag in her car, a drawstring from the hood of a jacket and a bungee cord. The drawstring was wrapped around her neck. The ribbon was wrapped once around her neck and oddly tied in a bow in the front. Her hair and body were also wet, although she was found on dry ground.

According to Detective Terry during the trial, "Her head was back towards the embankment. Her feet were near the river underneath some brush. Upon closer inspection, she was actually holding some of that brush in her hand. . . ." It was determined that this was the place where she was murdered and that she had not been transferred there.

Investigators began piecing together her movements before arriving at the river banks and determined it was likely that she headed down to the river banks to take pictures, as she was an avid photographer. Her brother Pavel said he "wasn't surprised she would go to such a remote spot. She was adventurous. She once hiked the Stampede Trail in Alaska with friends, searching for an abandoned bus made famous by Jon Krakauer's book Into the Wild."

Her camera was found in the trunk of her car, but there was not any film in it that could yield any clues about her death. Investigators quickly began interviewing people along the river to see if anyone had heard or seen anything out of the ordinary and came across two fishermen who were fishing about 100 yards from where Ira's body and car were discovered.

Mark Carver and Neil Cassada were cousins who grew up in the area and had been fishing in a new spot they had discovered the weekend before. This spot was about 100 yards from where Ira's car and body were discovered. Carver had been excited about the spot. He had returned to it because it did not require him to haul his boat to the river which was difficult for Carver to do since he suffers from carpal tunnel syndrome, a condition that makes his hands extremely weak.

His doctors recommended he not lift anything heavier than five pounds. Cassada also suffered from a heart condition, making it difficult to do anything too physical. Investigators questioned both men who reported that they had not seen Ira or had not heard anything from their fishing spot. They did report hearing a scraping sound that sounded like noise from construction.

They both willingly provided their DNA to investigators and went on their way. With the lack of forensic clues pointing toward any viable suspects, it was not until forensic analysis of the car several months later revealed partial DNA matches for Carver and Cassada that they became the prime suspects for Ira's murder. Mark Carver and Neal Cassada were arrested in December of 2008, seven months after her death and charged with conspiracy and murder. A day before Cassada's the trial began in 2010, Cassada died of a heart attack. Carver has always proclaimed their innocence.

"Simple" life of Mark Carver

Simple is the word often used to describe Mark Carver. "Simple in his routine, simple in his thought process, simple in his desires and wants," defense attorney Brent Ratchford said to reporters. Unlike Ira,

Carver is not well-educated and has limitations with writing and reading comprehension, which he has struggled with throughout most of his life.

At an early age, he was placed in special education classes because of these limitations and his relatively low IQ. At 16, he dropped out of school to work in a mill. At the time he was arrested, it was documented that he was taking medication prescribed for schizophrenia.

Carver is also the father of four children from two different marriages. "He lived for his children and family," his sister-in-law Robin Carver said when asked about him. "He didn't really do much of anything else. Fishing and hunting and family, that was about it."

Although his family speaks well of Carver, like most family members often do, he did have prior brushes with the law despite never being convicted of a crime. In 2005, Carver faced a charge of injury to property. Carver purportedly confronted two people he thought were stealing his four-wheeler. The charge was dismissed, and the file no longer exists. A year before Ira's murder, Carver accidentally shot his son. Carver and his son were supposedly wrestling when the gun went off. "It was an accident," his son said. The case was later dismissed and Carver never convicted of a crime.

Cassada also had had his own dealings with the law. In 1995, he was accused of assault and injury to personal property. He reportedly pointed a gun at someone. But the charges were dismissed and the details remain unclear.

His family insists that he had nothing to do with Ira's murder and that the stress of the trial for a crime he did not commit ultimately led to his death. Kaye Cassada, Neal Cassada's wife said "After 37 years of loving that man and being married to that man, I know he is not capable of hurting anybody. He would have died to help somebody." Charges against Cassada were dropped, a common proceeding with deceased suspects. His family attended the hearing and his son

Shannon Cassada said, "We want everybody to hear that he was an innocent man."

Carver also maintains his own innocence, stating "they said that they had ... my DNA and Neal's DNA in the car. I know that's a lie because Neal left, and they couldn't have gotten no DNA because I wasn't down there. I didn't go around it. I didn't go around the car. You know what I'm saying?" He also said he didn't think Cassada would commit such a crime because "He's got four young'uns himself."

Although lie detector tests are not reliable enough to be used in court, during the initial investigation Cassada took a polygraph test, which he passed. Because he passed, investigators did not give Carver one. Carver has been very vocal about his willingness to also take a polygraph test.

Touch DNA

During the investigation and trial, Carver never wavered in proclaiming his innocence and said this to Ira's family "I never seen her that day. If I'd knowed she was up there, I would have went up there and helped her. They could have easily come down and killed me just like they did her."

His trial began in 2010. Before the trial, Carver was offered a surprising plea deal from the prosecution: 4-8 years in prison if he pleaded guilty to second degree murder. Had he taken this deal and pled guilty to murder he could be out of prison and with his family. His attorney said, "I have never gotten such a low offer. And to me that spoke volumes about the case." Carver turned down this offer and prosecutors moved forward with the case.

Prosecutors argued that the two men killed Ira because she witnessed or photographed something they did not want her to see. As a result, they strangled her and pushed her car on the embankment where their DNA was transferred to the car. Their intention was to sink the car in the water, but it hit a stump where it stayed until it was finally discovered by the jet skiers. They then returned to their fishing spot until they were questioned by police.

Prosecutors relied on a relatively new forensic technique at the time known as "touch DNA." Unlike previous methods, touch DNA uses smaller amounts of DNA, such as skin cells transferred to a person or object when they come into contact with someone. But touch DNA is not as reliable as other DNA methods requiring blood or saliva because it is difficult to determine the origin of these cells. For instance, skin cells can be transferred indirectly by a third party or carrier.

For example, a man in California was falsely imprisoned because his DNA was found on a murder victim. It was determined that it was impossible that he was a killer because he had a solid alibi. At the time of the murder, he was unconscious in a hospital due to extreme intoxication.

Prosecutors then discovered that the same paramedic who treated him for intoxication was a first responder at the murder scene. The DNA from the intoxicated man was presumably transferred to the victim by the paramedic. This case set a precedent about the reliability of touch DNA and is cited by Carver's advocates for innocence as a possibility as to why Carver's and Cassada's DNA was found on Ira's car.

Despite this interesting theory, it was not presented by the defense in Carver's trial and the jury found him guilty of murder. He was sentenced to and is currently serving life in prison. Carver's advocates argue that the car and crime scene was not preserved, and that Carver and Cassada's DNA could have been transferred by officers or other people near the crime scene. Many officers, the jet skiers, first responders were all present at the crime scene and could have all inadvertently transferred the DNA to the car.

Several other inconsistencies exist in the prosecution's case. Carvers DNA was not found on her body nor on the trunk of the car where he and Cassada would have pushed it into the river bank according to prosecutors. Carvers DNA did not match a third DNA profile found on the bungee cord and the only DNA found under Ira's fingernails was her own.

His attorney and advocates also argue that the two men couldn't have physically pushed the car into the river bank due to Carver's carpal tunnel and Cassada's heart condition. Cassada supposedly got winded just walking. In 2013, Carver's attorneys filed an appeal on his behalf, but the appeals court determined "no error in the defendant's trial" occurred, meaning his conviction of life in prison would be upheld. But this did not deter his advocates from trying to prove Carver did not receive a fair defense during his trial.

Earlier this year, a judge granted the request of the North Carolina Actual Innocence Project, attorneys who have become interested in Carver case who believe Carver is wrongfully imprisoned, to see DNA reports that were never shared with Carvers defense team, along with further DNA testing.

They argue that Carver did not receive a proper defense as his lawyers did not call any witnesses or DNA experts to the stand and address the DNA evidence, and that the DNA evidence is not compelling enough beyond a reasonable doubt to warrant a life sentence for Carver. It is the only evidence linking Carver to the crime. Only time will determine the final outcomes of Carver's appeals as the evidentiary hearing has been postponed. Legal proceedings could take several years.

Other suspects

If Carver and Cassada's DNA was indeed transferred by a third party and they did not kill Ira, then who did? There was no one in her life that seemed to have any motive. Besides these two men, there was only one other suspect in her murder investigation. Nine months after the murder, Christopher Lemont Cooper wrote a letter to News anchor Erica Bryant to "confess a sin," that he and several other accomplices had killed Ira.

He said he drove a van full of friends that were all high and needed money for drugs. He said he was unable to sleep "because of what we did to that young woman." And wished to meet with the reporter. The TV station did not publish the letter and turned it over to investigators where they took the letter very seriously and launched an investigation with the North Carolina State Bureau of Investigations.

Police and investigators visited Cooper, where he was in jail on charges of rape, assault by strangulation, and for being delinquent in child support. He reportedly refused to cooperate with investigators, but they ultimately ruled him out as a suspect concluding that several of the accomplices he named were incarcerated at the time of the murder. They also cleared the other accomplices named in Cooper's letter and continued building their case against Carver and Cassada.

Free Mark Carver

Free Mark Carver is one of the prominent websites advocating for the release of Carver. They believe he is innocent or at the very least did not receive a proper defense in his trial. The website is run by a former newspaper journalist who now works in the fashion industry. She had no ties to the case or families and became intrigued with the case in 2011 after its details aired on Dateline NBC and through other online news articles.

One of the major theories from Carver's advocates presented on the website is that Ira was not murdered and in fact committed suicide by placing the ligatures around her neck herself. They claim that Ira was not the cheerful person described by her friends and loved ones and that she had battled depression.

Her boyfriend had broken up with her shortly before her murder and her poetry was sometimes dark and melancholy. The website alludes to accounts from unnamed people who claim that Ira had attempted suicide when she was younger and had seen a therapist at UNC Charlotte. The website does not provide sources and only mentions them as letters to the author.

Although this theory may be offensive to those who loved Ira and describe her as a happy and vibrant young woman, it has been addressed by pathologists who have dismissed this theory saying "For this to have been anything but a homicide, i.e., this was a suicide, this victim would have to tie three ligatures around her neck tightly and before death get into this position while that's going on and her legs underneath the brush given that position and I just feel like that was not consistent with what we are seeing. . . . Yes, and another thing that this illustrates a little bit better also is the presence of particular matter, soil and grass on her skirt as well. So that's another thing that would have had to happen. If this was a suicide she would have had to do all this stuff by herself. It is just not consistent with that theory."

Her brother Pavel, who has since completed his Ph.D. in biomedical engineering and continues to conduct research at a pediatric hospital, said he has read some of the internet theories about his sister's death, but they are "not grounded in reality." He asserts that his sister never attempted suicide and there was no indication she was depressed. Nevertheless, the fact remains that a lively, young woman lost her life just days after her 20th birthday.

Memorials

We may never know what really happened to Ira or why someone chose to take her life but it is clear that she touched many people who strive to keep her memory alive. The jet skiers who found her body, Dennis Lovelace and Brenda Pierce, placed a memorial cross where they found her car. The changing levels of the Catawba river sometimes covers part of the cross, but it is still visible to visitors.

A memorial bench as far as Alaska, where Ira spent a summer waitressing, also bears her name. "A Kansas City based artist Shane Blindt designed and installed this bench at the request of many co-workers whose lives were touched with Ira's presence during the 2007 McKinley Village Lodge summer season. Lettering on the memorial was hand drawn with pen showing the elegance and beauty of Ira's outward expressions contrasted with a raw and rugged placement into the world she left behind." It is maintained by locals there.

Her high school poetry team in Chapel Hill renamed the group The Sacrificial Poets in her honor.

What Time Devours is a book written by her former professor at UNC Charlotte who dedicated his book to her memory. He directed a campus production, which Ira was a part of the previous year before she was murdered. He also included a line from her poetry and her picture in the dedication of the book.

The controversy around her murder continues to intrigue people and several websites and pages are dedicated to outlining the details of the case. Ira's murder has been featured on Dateline and 20/20. She continues to captivate an almost cult following, and many people are still tirelessly working to prove that Carver is innocent and did not receive a fair trial. If this is the case, it means that justice has not been served for Ira and her family. But one thing is for sure, the memory of Ira Yarmolenko will continue to live on with her family, friends, and strangers that have been touched by her story.

THE DISAPPEARANCE OF KELSIE SCHELLING

ANA BENSON

Every time a woman goes missing or is found murdered, the police usually takes a closer look at their spouses or boyfriends. It is a standard procedure, especially if there were indications that they were in a troubled relationship. The disappearance of Kelsie Schelling is one of the biggest mysteries in Colorado. This young pregnant woman was last seen in February of 2013 and the case is still open to this day.

However, Kelsie's family was quite disappointed at the lack of interest by the police to investigate her then-boyfriend Donthe Lucas, who was clearly involved in this crime. After all, Donthe did invite Kelsie to his hometown on that fateful night and he was the last person who saw her alive. When they realized that the police are stalling with the investigation, the family made a promise that Kelsie's case will not be forgotten until they discover what really happened. They kept the public informed through their Facebook page and eventually managed to reach the Colorado Bureau of Investigation.

Early life

Kelsie Jean Schelling was born on 18th February 1991 in Holyoke, Colorado. She grew up in a tightknit family and later became even closer to her mother after the divorce of her parents. Kelsie was only eleven years old when they split up but she would often talk to her father as well. However, they didn't see each other that often because he moved to a different part of town. After graduating from high school, Kelsie attended Northeastern Junior College located in Sterling, Colorado. She was fascinated with psychology and planned to major in it once she gets accepted to the university.

Kelsie was friendly and outspoken, so it comes as no surprise that she had many friends and was a life of every party. During her time at Northeastern Junior College, Kelsie met Donthe Lucas. He was a star player on the basketball team and the two of them fell in love instantly. Donthe Lucas had a very difficult childhood and he grew up in Pueblo, Colorado which is an infamous place known for higher crime rates than anywhere else in the state. He loved basketball and it was clear that he would be an outstanding athlete even in high school. Basketball players do have enormous salaries so Donthe Lucas did see it as an opportunity to help his family out further down the line.

He was hoping that a scout would attend one of his games and recruit him for one of bigger colleges or universities that had a good basketball team. But his big break never happened. Instead, he ended up in Northeastern Junior College which was alright, but Donthe wasn't quite happy with that outcome. His dissatisfaction was evident even in the relationship with Kelsie. Their romance had constant ups and downs, and the two of them would break up, and get back together which drove Kelsie mad. They did finally call it quits after several semesters, and didn't see each other for quite some time.

After finishing the two years at the junior college, Kelsie pursued her education even further, and she moved to California to attend Vanguard University in Costa Mesa. She was finally able to study psychology full time. Donthe continued to play basketball for Emporia State University in Kansas. Kelsie's family was happy she managed to end her relationship with the troubled basketball player, and they hoped that she would make a new life far away from Colorado. Kelsie was independent and she enjoyed living and studying in California. When she wasn't attending classes, Kelsie worked at a tanning salon with her best friend. However, she did drop out of the college because the school work was a bit too much for her at the time and her only option was to go back home. She moved to Denver in 2012 and started working in a store. Meanwhile, Donthe Lucas was back in his hometown Pueblo.

The two of them started talking once again during the autumn of 2012. It was obvious that they still had feelings for each other, so no one was surprised when Donthe and Kelsie decided to spend the Christmas holidays together. The couple seemed happy to everyone around them, but Kelsie did tell her friends that their relationship was still very toxic. Donthe was still treating her badly, calling her names, and starting unnecessary fights. Soon enough everything will change. A few weeks after the holidays, Kelsie found out that she was pregnant. Shocked at first, Kelsie was lost and decided not to tell anyone for a couple of weeks. But keeping a secret was hard. So she called her mother and told her the news. Kelsie's mother Laura would later say that even though her daughter felt a bit stressed, she was still excited about the pregnancy. Yes, she was young but Kelsie was determined to make it work.

Donthe Lucas didn't take the news so well. Having in mind how dissatisfied he felt about his failed basketball career, it is not wrong to assume that the news about a baby simply solidified the fact that his dreams will never come true. Kelsie noticed the change in his mood and openly told him that he doesn't have to be a part of their baby's life. But it is also worth mentioning that Kelsie confided in her best friend that Donthe was ecstatic to become a father at one point. However, his mind was constantly changing. Kelsie went to see her doctor on 4th of February 2013 and he confirmed that she was eight weeks pregnant. The baby was healthy and doing well. The doctor provided her with an ultrasound of the unborn baby, and she was full of joy. Kelsie immediately sent out the pictures to her mother, her friends, and Donthe. Unfortunately, the excitement will not last forever.

The night of the disappearance

Donthe and Kelsey exchanged several emails on February 3rd, 2013. He invited her to visit him in Pueblo. She turned him down saying that she needs to go for a checkup the next day to make sure everything is alright with the baby. After seeing her doctor on the morning of February 4th, 2013, Kelsie went straight to the store. She worked the second shift and was expected to come home sometime after 10:00 PM that night. However, she was in contact with Donthe for the entire day, texting back and forth about the pregnancy. Donthe told her that she should drive out to Pueblo after work because he had a surprise for her. Not knowing what it is, Kelsie asked for more information because Pueblo is two hours away from Denver, and she would probably be tired after work. He insisted that she would be happy with his surprise and that he cannot tell her anything over the phone.

It is safe to assume that Kelsie thought that Donthe was ready to change and start a family with her. Their relationship wasn't a standard one but it seemed like Kelsie was willing to move past all the negative things and focus on the future. So after her shift ended, Kelsie got in her Chevy Cruze LTZ and drove to Pueblo in the middle of the night. Donthe was supposed to meet her in a parking lot in front of a local Walmart. The surveillance cameras did confirm that Kelsie got there on time, but Donthe was nowhere to be seen. She waited in a parked car for almost an hour before sending another text message to Donthe, saying that she has been in the parking lot for too long and that she would come pick him up at whatever location he is at the moment. She got a reply sometime around 12:15 AM.

Donthe told her that he will be waiting for her in the street next to his grandmother's home. Kelsie is seen exiting the parking lot a couple of minutes after she got the message. She clearly did arrive at the second rendezvous spot, but once again Donthe wasn't there. Kelsie sent him another message asking where is he and Donthe replied that he will be there in a minute. This is the last known communication between these two until sometime before 04:00 AM. After going through the phone records, police did discover that Donthe called Kelsie at 03:54 AM but she didn't pick up. The significance of this mysterious phone call will be revealed later. After reviewing the cell tower pings for both phones, the investigators did discover that they were in close proximity to each other.

The search for Kelsie

Kelsie's mother Laura got really worried the next day because she wasn't able to reach her daughter over the phone. She tried calling numerous times but it went straight to the voicemail. The last message she got from her daughter was the ultrasound image of her unborn child, and Laura wasn't sure if something happened to Kelsie after work, or she was ignoring her calls. Laura contacted Kelsie's friends who told her that she went to Pueblo to meet with Donthe. With no word from her daughter, she called Donthe who picked up his phone and told Laura that he had seen Kelsie last night, but that she drove back home in the morning.

Laura was starting to panic, but she did tell Donthe that she would involve the police if she doesn't hear from her daughter soon. Laura and Kelsie were very close and they did tell each other everything, but she suspected that her daughter kept this information from her because she didn't want Laura to know that she was meeting with Donthe. After all, Laura was aware of the nature of their relationship, and his reluctance to accept the baby. Plus, Laura would probably advise Kelsie not to go to Pueblo in the middle of the night.

Laura contacted the local law enforcement and told them that her daughter was missing. Without any solid leads or evidence, they started asking around for Kelsie. Their first step was to take a closer look at Donthe because he claimed that he was the last person to saw Kelsie. She did travel from Denver just to see him. After checking Kelsie's credit card records, they did notice that the card was used hours after Kelsie's last known contact with Donthe. They reviewed the surveillance of the ATM and noticed that Donthe had the card and picked up $400 from Kelsie's account. They weren't sure if Donthe had Kelsie's agreement to use the card, but that was a felony in the state of Colorado, so he was led to the police station for questioning. He had a lot of things to clear up, starting with the timeline of Kelsie's visit to Pueblo.

Donthe's interview

After being picked up by the police, Donthe told his own version of the story. They did see each other that night and talked until early morning hours. Donthe and Kelsie got into a fight and she felt too agitated to drive back home to Denver. She was also very tired from working the second shift. Instead, Kelsie decided to sleep in her car which was parked near his grandmother's house. According to Donthe, his phone rang sometime around 07:00 AM and it was Kelsie. She wasn't feeling well and asked Donthe to drive her to a hospital. He put on his clothes, got to her car, and drove her to the Parkview Hospital.

Kelsie wasn't sure if something happened to the baby during their argument last night and she insisted to see a doctor before she heads out to Denver. Donthe sat inside her car in the parking lot for two hours when she finally emerged from the hospital. Kelsie told him that she had lost the baby. She then asked Donthe to drive her to Walmart to get something to eat and buy some snacks for the road. The two of them started fighting while they were in Walmart and Kelsie refused to drive him home. Donthe simply walked away and got to his grandmother's house on foot. He didn't see Kelsie later in the day and he assumed she went home. He didn't mention stopping at the ATM to pick up the money during his initial interview.

The investigators did notice a couple of possible leads that could collaborate Donthe's story, namely the Parkview Hospital. Each medical facility keeps detailed records of the patients they treat. After speaking to the staff and going through the data, they have confirmed that Kelsie didn't check in during the morning of February 5th. There were also numerous surveillance cameras all over the building and none of them picked up Kelsie entering or leaving the hospital. It was obvious that this part of Donthe's story was not true.

Of course, the police investigators decided to check out Walmart as well because the parking lot and stores do have surveillance cameras, and they might have picked up something that would be of use. While they couldn't find Kelsie or Donthe entering the Walmart, they did notice Kelsie's car on the parking lot. However, the timeline didn't match up with Donthe's story because Kelsie's car appeared at noon, and not in the morning. Plus, Donthe was the only passenger in the car.

Another surveillance camera which was positioned on the back side of Walmart did record Donthe getting into his mother's car – another detail he failed to mention in the initial talk with the investigators.

Without any proof that Donthe's version of the events is true, they called him up for a second interview. The investigators did have a plan this time - they wanted to find out more about the ATM, and how it fits into his timeline. He told the detectives that he took $400 in order to pay his bills and that Kelsie lent him the money since he was at the ATM while Kelsie was at the hospital. When the detectives told Donthe that there is no record of Kelsie ever being in that hospital, his reply was: "I don't even know what to say right now."

They also presented him with Walmart surveillance video that proves Donthe was the only person in the car. He was surprised with the evidence put in front of him, and before the detectives managed to get him to open up, he decided to lawyer up. He was only charged with the identity theft due to the fact that he used Kelsie's credit card, but the case was dropped. The judge had determined that Donthe did use Kelsie's credit card in the past and it was a normal behavior. However, nobody managed to figure out why Donthe had her card in the first place. After all, if Kelsie decided to ran away and start a new life, she would need the money, as well as her vehicle.

Speaking of Kelsie's car, the investigators took a closer look at the surveillance video from Walmart parking lot because they wanted to follow the vehicle. Exactly one day after Donthe left Kelsie's car there, another man approached the car and got inside by using the key. He didn't break in or steal the car. The man was dressed in black, wearing a hoodie, so identifying him was almost impossible. His body type was different than Donthe's, and the mystery man was significantly shorter. Keep in mind that Donthe was a tall basketball player, so his height would be noticeable, even in a low-quality video.

Seeing the direction in which the car went, the police collected the surveillance videos from stores and businesses which were in close proximity. They put the puzzle pieces together and found a route but they couldn't follow it all the way. One day later, the car was dropped at the parking lot of Saint Mary Corwin Hospital. The man locked the car and walked away. The investigators located the vehicle on 14th of February, 2013 and figured out the timeline. But nobody knows where the car was during 6th of February. There weren't any signs of a struggle that would indicate that Kelsie was killed in her car. Almost all of her personal items were missing, including her wallet and a backpack.

While it is unclear if the vehicle was tested for the traces of DNA, an unnamed police officer who worked for Pueblo Police Department will later say that they did find bodily fluids in the trunk of Kelsie's car, as well as two palm prints. However, no one knows what happened with this evidence and was it ever tested. It is simply another thing which the police investigators decided to ignore in this case. Unfortunately, the whole investigation will be under scrutiny soon after.

Theories

Figuring out a solid theory without too many evidence or information can be challenging. Laura, Kelsie's mother, claims that her daughter was probably murdered and that it was premeditated. The first red flag for her was Donthe's initial invitation to meet him before the doctor's appointment. When Kelsie refused, he knew that he had to act fast. Donthe lured Kelsie to Pueblo by saying that he has something to show her, but he never gave an explanation to the law enforcement about what the surprise really was.

It is clear that Kelsie was alive and well up until the point she met Donthe in the street next to his grandmother's house. This is where the trail goes cold. The activity on her phone stops until 04:00 AM. If we analyze the location of the phones, another theory is that Donthe led Kelsie to a remote location and harmed her. It was possible that Kelsie dropped her phone in the middle of a struggle. Donthe couldn't find the phone in the dark, so he had to call her number. He was very likely getting rid of the evidence.

There is a possibility that the two of them did indeed get into a fight, and that an unfortunate accident happened. However, it is more likely that Donthe planned to get rid of Kelsie, and had planned every single step he would take that night. He really insisted to see her as soon as possible. While it is not fair to put the blame on the rest of Lucas family, the fact that his mother picked him up immediately after he left Kelsie's vehicle at the Walmart's parking lot indicates that she knew what was going on. Pueblo Police Department did stop investigating Donthe, and they claimed they didn't have enough physical evidence to prove that a crime really occurred. But they did receive a couple of noteworthy tips which were ignored and never pursued.

The missed opportunities

The entire investigation of the disappearance of Kelsie Schelling was troubling from the very beginning. While the detectives did not have physical evidence of a crime, it was clear that Donthe was the last person who saw Kelsie alive. In every standard investigation, he would have been the prime suspect, and the investigators would do their best to find more proof that he was somehow connected to the crime. The cell tower pings did show that both of their phones were in a remote area next to Pueblo in the early morning hours.

But there are even bigger missed opportunities that could have provided the investigators with the proof they needed. For instance, Donthe was living in his grandmother's house at the time of Kelsie's disappearance. However, the entire family moved out soon after. The landlord started redecorating the house because he wanted to rent it again. He did hear about the missing girl from Denver but had no idea about the details of the case, or the fact that the Lucas family was involved in any way.

He decided to put the new carpets in and when he lifted the old one, the landlord noticed a strange stain on the bottom. He contacted the police enforcement because he was worried that something bad has happened in the house. However, the police ignored his request to check out the stained carpet, and no one had ever arrived at Lucas' previous residence to pick it up. The landlord ended up throwing the carpet away because he simply couldn't keep it forever in the house and wanted to move on with the renovation.

Another missed opportunity involved a couple of fishermen who were out on a lake on a night fishing expedition. It is important to mention that the lake was located near the Saint Mary Corwin Hospital. As you might recall, that was the spot where the police officers discovered Kelsie's vehicle on the 14th of February 2013. They were out on a bank when a hook got stuck to something poking out of the sand. The fishermen went to investigate and were sure that they saw a part of a human ribcage, as well as a skull.

They were terrified by that discovery and left the area right away. Both of them were reluctant to notify the police because they did have some troubles with the law in the past. But that didn't stop them from telling this story to their friends who urged them to contact the local law enforcement. A couple of months passed before they finally talked to the police, but the lake wasn't searched afterward.

The current searches

Family and friends continued to search for Kelsie even after it was clear that the police enforcement forgot about her case. They created a Facebook group that was constantly updated with new information. Pueblo Police Department did go through many changes after Kelsie went missing. The lead investigator was replaced with a new one who was willing to cooperate with the Schelling family. The Schellings did offer a large reward for any new leads that might help them locate their missing daughter. The reward was $100,000 at one point.

This eventually led to false claims and misleading messages such as the one which claimed that Kelsie was still alive, but was placed into a sex traffic ring after a hired hitman decided not to kill her.

Laura Schelling contacted the police and told them about the message. Since the investigators decided to follow every lead possible, they dug deeper and even involved the FBI. Their experts did manage to trace the message back to Russia through the IP address so it was clear that this tip was useless.

The biggest break in the case happened in the spring of 2017 when Colorado Bureau of Investigation finally got the authorization from the local law enforcement to join the search. CBI did determine that the prime suspect should be Donthe Lucas, and they got the warrant to search the area around his previous place of residence. A large number of police officers was seen around that house during April of 2017, and they dug up the parts of the backyard using heavy machinery.

The search has been successful and the officers left the scene carrying bags of evidence. However, they stated that they didn't find any traces of Kelsie's remains. Kelsie's family released the following statement after the search: "The past 2 days have been grueling and emotional, ending with the outcome we did not hope for. Kelsie is still missing. There is no way for me to convey to you all the pain that I feel right now. Sincere, heartfelt thanks goes out to the members of Pueblo PD, CBI and Parks & Rec who worked so hard on this search for Kelsie. This was a physically demanding excavation for them and we witnessed how hard they worked. Despite all the issues we have had in the past, the new leadership over Kelsie's case from PPD and active involvement from CBI is giving us hope that an effective investigation is finally taking place."

The case is still active and the police didn't arrest Donthe. But the positive changes are happening and Kelsie's family is certain that they will find the answers they are looking for now that the investigation is finally moving forward.

FINDING JENNIFER : THE DISAPPEARANCE OF JENNIFER KESSE

 EMILY LOVATO

MARY DANIELLE TAYLOR

<u>FOR A COMPLETE LISTING OF TRUE CRIME STORIES</u>

The unsolved disappearance of Jennifer Kesse from her Orlando, Florida condo in the early hours of January 23, 2006, garnered widespread attention from the local and national media alike, leading to large-scale search parties conducted by the Orlando Police Department and FBI. However, despite the fact that Jennifer Kesse disappeared over ten years ago in the parking lot of her apartment complex, investigators are no closer to solving the case.

Jennifer Kesse, a finance manager for a Florida property and vacation company, had left her recently purchased condo in Orlando, Florida to begin her morning commute to work. However, Jennifer would never make it into work that morning, and her family and friends would never hear from her again. Read on to learn more about who Jennifer Kesse was, about the circumstances of her disappearance, and the local and national reaction to her missing persons case.

Early Life

Jennifer Kesse, a graduate of Vivian Gaither High School in Tampa, Florida, had graduated with a degree in finance from the University of Central Florida, located in Orlando, Florida, in 2003, where she also served as a member of the Alpha Delta Pi sorority. Following her graduation from college, Jennifer began working at the Central Florida Investments Timeshare Company as a finance manager.

Shortly before the date of her disappearance, Jennifer and her current boyfriend had visited Saint Croix, in the U.S. Virgin Islands, for a vacation. After returning home from the Virgin Islands by plane, Jennifer drove directly from her boyfriend's house in South Florida to her job in Ocoee, Florida for a full day of work. Jennifer would return home to her newly-purchased condo in Orlando that evening, the very same evening of her disappearance.

Night of Her Disappearance

Jennifer was last seen leaving the Westgate Resorts office of the Central Florida Investments Timeshare Company on the night of January 23, 2006 in Ocoee, Florida, after returning home from her vacation in Saint Croix, in the U.S. Virgin Islands, with her boyfriend. Several close friends and members of her family received calls from Jennifer that night, and the last call that she made before her disappearance was to her boyfriend shortly before 10:00pm.

Jennifer typically called or texted her boyfriend during her morning commute to work to wish him good morning; however, he became concerned on the morning of January 24th when he did not receive a message from her. When he attempted to call Jennifer that morning, his call was sent directly to voicemail. Because Jennifer had previously told him that she had an early-morning meeting at work, he assumed that she was busy and would call him once she received his voicemail. He continued his day at work until receiving a call from Jennifer's parents later that day informing him that she had never made it to work.

When Jennifer did not show up to work or contact her direct supervisor, a coworker contacted Jennifer's parents to express concern and see if they had heard from her. Jennifer was supposed to attend a very important work meeting with her higher-ups that morning, and it was extremely unlike her to fail to show up with calling ahead. Upon receiving the call from Jennifer's office, her parents immediately jumped into action. Her father, Drew Kesse, said "We were calling hospitals, calling jails, calling her friends, asking them to call places, calling Rob, and he tried calling her and she did not answer."

Her parents soon jumped into their car and made the two-hour drive to Jennifer's condo in Orlando, Florida from their home in Tampa. While driving, her parents contact her condo management office at *Mosaic Apartments*, located on the 3700 block Convoy Road in Orlando, and requested that the manager stop by her condo to check on her. He reported that she was not home, that her condo was in great condition, and that her car was not in the parking lot.

In addition, once her parents arrived in Orlando and entered their daughter's condo, they did not notice anything out of place or any signs of a struggle. Furthermore, they noticed that Jennifer's clothes were laid out on her bed and that a wet towel was present in the restroom, leading them to believe that Jennifer was at home that morning. Her father Drew later said, "We actually found two or three outfits laid out on her bed she was picking. Showered, shower was still damp. Her towel was still damp. Her work stuff was not there. So we knew that, OK, she got ready for work."

The parents quickly contacted the Orlando police department to report her as missing. Family members began passing out flyers that evening and reaching out to local media organizations, while the local police department began organizing a search party.

A local television reporter and friend of Jennifer's, Scott Thuman, described the family's actions like this: "I made sure they were on every TV station every single night as long as we could keep that alive. They did the networks, they did radio shows. They did every newspaper interview they could." An investigative reporter who covered the case would later say, "It was hard to go anywhere without seeing her face and her picture and also the information on her vehicle."

Timeline

January 23, 2006

Early Morning – Leaves her boyfriend's home in Central Florida to head directly to her office at Westgate Resorts for a full day at work. Jennifer and her boyfriend had just returned from a trip to Saint Croix, U.S. Virgin Islands.

6:00pm – Jennifer leaves her office at Westgate Resorts and drives to her condo complex in Orlando, Florida. She unpacks her clothes and contacts several family members to let them know that she has returned home from vacation safely.

10:00pm – Jennifer calls her boyfriend and speaks with him for several minutes before saying goodnight. Jennifer's boyfriend is the last known person to speak with her before her disappearance.

January 24, 2006

7:30am – Police believe that Jennifer was abducted sometime around 7:30am to 8:00am on the morning of the 24th. She was likely taken either while walking through the parking lot towards her car or while entering her vehicle.

8:30am – Jennifer's boyfriend calls her, but the call is sent directly to voicemail. Jennifer typically calls her boyfriend during her morning commute to say good morning and chat. He assumes that she is busy with an early-morning meeting that they had previously discussed.

11:00am – Jennifer's coworkers, concerned that she uncharacteristically did not show up to work and had missed a very important meeting, called her parents to see if Jennifer is okay. Both her parents and coworkers realize that something is wrong.

11:15am – Jennifer's parents immediately begin the two-hour drive to Jennifer's condo in Orlando from their home in Tampa. Her parents contact her condo's management office and request that they enter her condo to check on her. He reports that nothing is out of the ordinary and that her car is gone.

12:00pm – Jennifer's brother, who lives locally, arrives at her condo complex and begins looking for her. Unbeknownst to anyone at the time, a surveillance camera at an apartment complex 1 mile down the road from her own condo shows an unidentifiable man parking Jennifer's car. The video shows the suspect parking the car, and sitting in it for approximately 30 seconds before exiting the car and walking away from the complex. Unfortunately for investigators, the suspect's face was obscured by a fencing post and neither the local police department nor the FBI were able to produce a useable shot of the suspect's face.

1:00pm – Jennifer's parents arrive in Orlando and immediately enter her condo. They notice that her shower is covered with water and that her towel is still wet. They also see that her work clothes are laid out on her unmade bed, that her makeup and hairdryer are lying out on her bathroom sink, and that her pajamas are piled on the restroom floor. Police theorize that Jennifer may have had a fight with her boyfriend and left her apartment to cool off. They preach patience to the parents.

5:00pm – Jennifer's close family and friends begin passing out missing persons flyers to local passerby. The police respond by sending a detective to her condo to gather information and investigate her disappearance. Police begin to question her family and friends, and begin to organize a search party.

January 26, 2006

8:10am – After seeing a report on Jennifer's disappearance on the local news, a resident at a local apartment complex calls the Orlando Police Department to report that her car has been parked in their complex for the last two days. Police arrive at the complex to verify this report, and quickly haul the car away to local police facilities for a forensic analysis. Police are finally able to identify and locate security footage showing an unidentified person parking Jennifer's car and leaving the complex by foot. This footage would lead investigators to determine that Jennifer may have been abducted.

Investigation

Jennifer's parents, as well as the initial investigators who looked into her case, noticed that Jennifer's apartment showed no signs of forced entry, her condo door was locked, and there were no signs of a struggle. Furthermore, because Jennifer's work clothes were laid out neatly and there was evidence that she had recently showered, investigators theorized that she had gotten ready for work the morning of her disappearance and had left her condo to begin her morning commute. The also assert that Jennifer likely left her apartment and was abducted either during the walk to her car or as she was entering the vehicle.

Two days after Jennifer's disappearance on January 26th, her 2004 black Chevy Malibu was located at the *Huntington on the Green* apartment complex, located at Americana Ave. and Texas, a little over a mile away from her own condo. While the apartment complex her car was parked at did have several security cameras, covering both her car and the exit to the apartment complex itself, the videos offered limited clues to her disappearance.

The video showed a "person of interest" who dropped off her car at noon the day of her disappearance; however, the best shots from the video were rendered useless since fencing from the apartment complex concealed the face of the unidentified man in three separate frames. The suspect was seen wearing an all-white uniform, leading some close to the case to believe that the suspect was a painter or other type of manual laborer.

Beau Zimmer, an investigative reporter who followed Jennifer Kesse's disappearance, described the video like this: "There's two different angles, all surrounding the pool area. But it's very, very blurry and it's hard to see. But you can see someone pulling Jennifer's car into that visitor's parking lot. They wait inside the car for a number of seconds before they get out and look around, and then walk out of frame of the picture. But the next shot of the video was what everyone thought would be so helpful. The next shot was of a person that was walking back and forth along the fence line."

However, he noted, "Every frame of the video, the person is obscured by a post and so you never see the person's face." Zimmer would later remark, "It has got to be the most frustrating thing for detectives, the most frustrating thing for the Kesse family, because for just one split second, later or earlier, you would have seen that individual's face and you would have had a better idea of what happened to Jennifer."

When investigators shared footage from the video with Jennifer's family and friends, they were unable to identify the man in question. A Fox News reporter would later say in a televised retrospective segment on the case that the obscured image made the man the "luckiest person of interest ever."

Both the FBI and NASA were called in to conduct advanced video analyses of the footage to provide more clues on the stalled case. The FBI determined that the person was roughly 5'3" to 5'5" tall, but could not offer definitive proof of the suspect's gender. Despite NASA's digital enhancement of the video, they were not able to provide any additional information that could help the case.

Despite the dead-end that the surveillance video represented, investigators were able to put together several pieces of the puzzle. Since all of Jennifer's valuables were found in her car, parked a mile down the street in a different apartment complex, they were able to determine that robbery was not a primary motive in her disappearance. In addition, a police dog was able to track a scent a full mile from her parked car back to her condo complex, leading investigators to theorize that the unidentified suspect returned to her complex directly after disposing of her car. However, police were unable to locate any helpful evidence along the route walked by the suspect.

After conducted a search and forensic analysis of her vehicle, investigators identified two pieces of evidence: a latent fingerprint from an unidentified individual and a small strand of DNA. Given the lack of evidence found in the car, coupled with the lack of clothing fibers, hair strands, and DNA, the police believe that the car was thoroughly wiped down in an attempt to remove incriminating evidence. The investigative reporter assigned to the case, Beau Zimmer, would say, "There was maybe one print and detectives think that it was maybe wiped down, and that this was an intentional act to not only hide this vehicle, but also to hide any evidence of who may have driven it."

Despite the lack of evidence found in her car, investigators did notice that several items were missing. They were unable to located her cell phone, keys, purse, clothes, briefcase, or iPod. While police are often able to track a missing person's cell phone or bank accounts for clues, her bank account was never accessed by her captors and her cell phone remained turned off with the battery removed.

Investigators quickly compiled a list of potential suspects after questioning her friends and family for clues. Her current boyfriend was questioned and quickly eliminated from the list of suspects after providing a valid alibi. In addition, Jennifer's ex-boyfriend and one of her coworkers, who had romantic feelings for Jennifer and had sought a relationship with her in the past, were interviewed by the police.

One the of the most interesting factors in Jennifer's disappearance was the fact that her condo complex was undergoing major construction at the time of her disappearance. Many of the workers, some who were undocumented immigrants, were living in the complex while it was undergoing construction. Jennifer had mentioned her discomfort with some of the workers to her family on multiple occasions, claiming that they harassed and catcalled her regularly. Jennifer's parents have also stated on multiple occasions that they believe she may have been a victim of human trafficking.

In May 2007, the CEO of Central Florida Investments Timeshare Company, David Siegel, offered a $1 million reward for information that led to her being found alive; however, the reward was never claimed. A $5,000 reward for information on her disappearance, offered by the Central Florida Crime line, remains active today.

Suspects

Ex-boyfriend

Jennifer had recently broken up with a previous boyfriend, and he was reportedly very angry about the breakup and the fact that Jennifer was now dating another man. Beau Zimmer would report that Jennifer's ex-boyfriend became incredibly angry after finding out that she was travelling to Saint Croix with Rob, saying "The night before or sometime before, he had been out drinking and gotten drunk and apparently he was upset that he was not the one that was with Jennifer.

Zimmer would later remark that the ex-boyfriend was cleared by the police, saying "They talked with him several times, and while police say he is not a suspect in the case, certainly you get the feeling from others that he should be talked to a little bit more."

Current Boyfriend

Jennifer's boyfriend, Rob, was initially considered a suspect in her disappearance. The couple had just returned from a vacation in Saint Croix, in the U.S. Virgin Islands, and Rob was the last person who had spoken with Jennifer the night before her disappearance. Police soon interviewed Rob to learn more about his relationship with Jennifer and to ascertain his whereabouts the morning of her disappearance.

However, Rob was quickly discounted as a suspected. Rob had an airtight alibi; he was more than 200 miles away when Jennifer was abducted, at his home in Fort Lauderdale, Florida. Investigative journalist Beau Zimmer says, "The police said that between his phone records and the fact that he was in South Florida, we don't believe that he was involved."

The police department's belief in Rob's innocence is shared by Jennifer's family. He was fully cooperative with the police department and FBI's investigation and willingly provided a DNA sample twice. Jennifer's father, Drew Kesse, said "Rob has been put over the coals, Rob has been polygraphed three of four times, Rob has been interviewed probably over a dozen times."

Coworker

Both Jennifer's family, friends, and coworkers reported that Jennifer had recently turned down a coworker who was hitting on her and attempting to strike up a romantic relationship. Jennifer's mom, Joyce, said that the coworker was married and was refusing to accept Jennifer's decision not to date him, both because he was married and because she did not date people she worked with. Joyce later said, "Jennifer arranged to meet him in the cafeteria at work so that once and for all she could tell him, 'Leave me alone, I am never going to date you. And besides, I don't date married men.'"

The police department did question Jennifer's coworker and eventually eliminated him from the list of suspects. However, Joyce said "We feel it should have been consistent to keep the pressure on that individual."

Construction Workers

Jennifer, who had just purchased and moved into her newly renovated condo two months before her disappearance, had repeatedly expressed concern about construction workers in her complex. The complex, which was undergoing extensive renovations at the time, was housing undocumented immigrants working on the consecution projects, at the time of her disappearance. Beau Zimmer has stated, "Jennifer told some of her friends that she felt really uncomfortable around some of these guys. Apparently there may have been some cat calls and things like that."

Jennifer's parents have also stated that she may have been abducted by a construction worker, with her mother saying, "I can't help wonder if someone was stalking her from afar that she didn't even know. Could there have been someone watching her comings and goings?"

The local police department did question many of the construction workers who were working at her condo complex at the time of her disappearance; however, no leads would develop from this line of questioning. Zimmer would say, "The police tried to talk to as many of the workers that would have been there when Jennifer disappeared, but they acknowledge that they may have missed some people."

Sex Traffickers

Drew Kesse has claimed that it is well-known that there was an active sex trafficking ring in the Orlando area at the time of Jennifer's disappearance, which her parents think may be linked to her abduction. Jennifer's father, Drew Kesse, has stated "My gut feeling to this day, honestly, I truly believe she was trafficked." His sentiment was echoed by Jennifer's close friend and local television reporter Scott Thuman, was said "It would make sense on a lot of levels, as unfortunate as it is."

Reaction

The disappearance of Jennifer Kesse led to nationwide outrage and attention, with coverage in the local, state, national, and international media. At the behest of Orlando Police Department chief Val Demings, the FBI took over control of the case on June 10, 2010 and remains in-charge of her missing persons case to this day. She remains on the FBI's Missing List and they continue to search for her and react to current leads, with the most recent search taking place in February 2014. She is also still considered still missing by the Orlando Police Department, Interpol, and the Orange County, Florida Police Department.

In reaction to Jennifer's disappearance and the investigation into her disappearance. The Florida House of Representatives passed Senate Bill 502, entitled "The Jennifer Kesse and Tiffany Sessions Missing Persons Act," by unanimous vote on May 2, 2008. This bill changed the way that missing persons cases are handled in the state of Florida, instituting reforms such as allowing the Florida Department of Law Enforcement to provide assistance in missing persons cases involving adults. Prior to the passage of this law, the FDLE was limited in its ability to provide assistance in cases involving the disappearance or abduction of adults aged 26 or older.

JODI HUISENTRUIT

Jodi Sue Huisentruit was a news anchor for KIMT, a station based in Mason City, Iowa. On June 27th, 1995, she called the station and told her co-worker that she was on her way to work after she overslept.

It would be the last time anyone heard from her.

There were signs of a struggle outside of her apartment indicating that she had been abducted. She would disappear without a trace. Numerous rumors and "persons of interest" have emerged but no official suspect has ever been named.

Over twenty years later, the question still remains.

What happened to Jodi Huisentruit?

EARLY LIFE

Jodi was born in Long Prairie, Minnesota, the youngest daughter of Maurice Huisentruit and Imogene "Jane" Huisentruit. Her father would pass away at age sixty-two of colon cancer. Jodi was only fourteen at the time.

Jodi was an excellent student who also excelled at golf. She would lead her high school team to victory in the state Class A tournament in 1985 and 1986. After high school, she would attend St. Cloud State University where she majored in TV Broadcasting and Speech Communication.

After graduating college, she worked for Northwest Airlines as a stewardess until she landed her first broadcasting gig at KGAN in Cedar Rapids, Iowa. She then briefly returned to Minnesota to work at KSAX before relocating to Iowa for a job at KIMT.

Jodi was well-liked at the station and immediately became a hit with her viewers who liked the infectious enthusiasm of the sunny blonde. She was petite, blonde and had a made for television smile.

Family members, however, would often worry about Jodi as they perceived her as a bit naïve.

"She would befriend anyone," investigative reporter Steve Powell said. "It was part of her nature and that is what made her a popular fixture at the station. In some of her family home videos, you can see the playfulness of her nature. She was outgoing and bubbly. Not the type of person who made enemies."

"I hired Jodi," said Doug Merbach, former news director of KIMT. "I brought her to Mason City. Could there have been something we could have warned her about and talked to her about? I don't know. What do you think happened? I've been asked that so many times. I feel as ignorant as the next person. I just don't know. I don't want to point fingers at anybody without looking inside the investigation and opening up those books. I don't know. I think it had to be somebody who knew her. I think it had to be somebody who had an emotional response to something Jodi said or did that caused them to do that. I don't think it was random - I don't think it was planned. I think it was planned to a certain extent - but not days and weeks ahead of time."

"She had so much enthusiasm," her best friend at the station, Robin Woflram said. "Every day was a gift and treated as something to explore. Sometimes occasionally she would call, I mean this girl got up at 3 am, and she said 'What are you doing after work?' It's like 10:30 pm and I'd tell her that I'm going home and going to bed. She'd say, 'Oh, Robin, there's plenty of time to sleep. Life is for the living.' And she embraced every single moment."

"It's sometimes difficult to get close - especially women - in this industry because you're always looking over your shoulder and wondering if someone is coming up behind me. I'll never forget the first day she walked in and her laugh. She'll always be remembered for that. She's fun and spunky. I think I'll like her. She's got zest for living."

JODI IS MISSING

Huisentruit would play in a golf tournament the day before she disappeared. She then went to the home of John Vansice and according to him, they watched a videotape of her birthday party that he had arranged for her.

On June 27th, 1995, KIMT producer Amy Kuns noticed that Jodi still had not reported for work. She called her at the apartment and explained that she had overslept.

"I'm on my way," Jodi said.

Two hours later, Jodi still had not arrived at the station.

Kuns would substitute for her on her morning show Daybreak.

An hour later, she would call the Mason City police.

"It became known only after that Jodi wasn't always punctual," Powell said. "A lot of her co-workers covered for her because they didn't want her to get in trouble with the brass at the station. So, her arriving late wasn't that much of an unusual occurrence. Not showing up at all certainly was, however, and they called for the police to do a welfare check."

Police would arrive at Jodi's apartment and find her red Mazda Miata still parked in the apartment lot. There was evidence suggesting that there had been a struggle near her car.

Jodi's keys were stuck in the driver side door, broken in half. Her blow dryer, jewelry, and red high heels were strewn about in the parking lot.

The top of her convertible was dented. Blood and tissue was splattered on the driver side mirror. Skid marks on the pavement suggested that she had been dragged to a waiting vehicle."

"The scene suggested that she had been grabbed while putting her keys in the car door," Powell said. "She was in a rush, having overslept for whatever reason. Was probably going to make herself up on the way to the station when someone rushed up behind her."

There was a palm print left behind on her car which police were never able to identify.

MORNING SCREAMS

Police would inquire with neighbors and found three tenants who stated that they heard screams in the early morning hours. Another neighbor reported seeing a white van with lights on parked nearby Jodi's vehicle.

Three months after her disappearance, Jodi's family would hire private investigators from McCarthy and Associates (MAIS) in Minneapolis who then worked in tandem with another private investigator, Doug Jasa.

"A lot of things struck me about the case," Jasa said. "I still remember all of the cards they found in Jodi's apartment. They were birthday cards. I think there were 50 of them and we're reading through them - reading through them. People had written very nice notes in the birthday cards. We went door to door in the apartment complex - talking with different residences about what they heard. One lady remembers specifically looking at her clock when she heard the scream."

Her family held out hope throughout the harrowing ordeal.

"I couldn't have had a better kid sister," Jodi's older sister Joanne Nathe said. "She tried to motivate me. What are your goals? That makes me stronger. It's a nightmare...not knowing where she is. We were hoping to find her in the first few months."

Neither the police nor the private investigators would come up with any evidence. All they had were more questions.

Questions that would forever remain unanswered.

"What caused her to sleep in that day," Officer Terrance Prochaska with Mason City Police Department asked. "What caused her to answer the phone and rush into work? What was she doing the night before? We all want to know the fine details. We know where she was at. She was golfing. She had driven home and made a phone call to her friend. Those are facts. But its' that gray area in between that we don't understand."

Rumors would plague the investigation as numerous false hopes and bizarre allegations were made. Mason City had a growing drug problem and some speculated that Jodi was working on a story to expose drug dealers. This was an outlandish claim considering that Jodi was not an investigative reporter and was not trained for that discipline. KIMT was a call-in television station. They got their news from the wires and reported it after some fact-checking. Another unfounded rumor came from a disgruntled female police officer who claimed that two of her fellow officers were responsible for Jodi's disappearance. Again, these were uncorroborated allegations and the officer spreading the rumors was terminated.

The community at large would get involved and in May of 1996, over one hundred volunteers searched the area of Cerro Gordo County. They would leave flags in the ground to mark anything they found to be suspicious. Authorities would then comb through the area but no further evidence was ever found.

Over one thousand interviews were conducted after her disappearance. Not one single suspect ever emerged.

Police initially turned their attention to the last person to have seen Jodi alive.

John Vansice.

Vansice was a lifelong Iowa native and lived in Newton where he was married with two children. He divorced in the early 1990s and moved to the Key Apartments in Mason City where he would befriend Jodi.

Jodi would reportedly spend a lot of time with the fifty-year-old Vansice. He was more than twenty years her senior and seemed to be "obsessed" with her. He threw around more money than his listed occupation (corn seeder) would suggest he could afford as he purchased a $26,000 boat in 1995 which he named "Jodi".

Jodi's purchase of the Mazda Miata seemed fishy as well as the car was more expensive than her meager salary as a broadcaster would allow.

STRANGER OR STALKER?

"I was the last to see her alive," Vansice said as he approached law enforcement officers investigating Jodi's apartment. He told police of what happened the night before, that Jodi was at his apartment watching a birthday video.

Vansice had taken special care in throwing Jodi a birthday party. He had printed out the invites himself, making sure his name was printed on the bottom with the words "a party given by John Vansice and friends."

Joann described Vansice as being "fixated" on her sister but stated that Jodi never mentioned anything about him during their conversations. She did mention Vansice in conversations with her mother and alluded to the fact that he may be developing a romantic interest in her. She also stated that she felt "uncomfortable" during a recent breakfast she had with Vansice.

Joann would describe a meeting she had with Vansice in which she thought his behavior was "cold" and "unfriendly." She asked Vansice if Jodi ever mentioned their Dad to him and he abruptly ended their conversation.

During his public appearances, Vansice seemed calm in relaying his support for Jodi's return.

Too calm.

"We're all praying and hoping that she's okay," Vansice said. "We just have to keep praying and keep hoping and I'll think she'll come back. I really do."

"I liked Jodi so much I named my boat after her," Vansice said when asked by a reporter why he named his boat after her. "She was such a big part of my life and she just made me feel so good."

Jodi's friend, Tammy Baker, once asked Jodi point blank if she was involved with Vansice.

"Absolutely not," Jodi said.

"Vansice was questioned by police but ruled out as he passed the lie detector tests," Powell said. "But any sociopath can pass a lie detector test. Vansice should have been suspect number one on the basis of telling the police that he 'was the last one to see her alive.' Making a statement like that, with no dead body found, is a revealing disclosure."

Most people close to the case believe that Vansice is involved but never directly say his name as if they are afraid.

"It is a head scratcher as to why the police didn't come at him harder," Powell said. "It was almost as if there was a veil of secrecy over his relationship with Jodi and what it exactly entailed. I believe that it may have been in part to protect Jodi's reputation. She was an All-American girl, church-raised and church-going. But the question had to be asked of what her relationship with Vansice exactly was or more specifically, what did he have in mind? Did he want to be her older sugar daddy? He bought her gifts, gave her birthday parties, making deposits in the account so to speak. But when he finally came to collect did she rebuff his advances and spur him to murderous anger?"

"What is certain is that he was her neighbor and they would hang out a lot. When they looked into her apartment they would find four cans of sixteen-ounce beers. No way the petite Jodi could handle that and then head off to work. The toilet seat was up. The other thing missing from her apartment was her personal notebook. Most sexual predators wouldn't steal something like that. But again, hindsight is 20/20 and they should have made a beeline for Vansice's boat the moment they found out that he named his boat after a woman whom he supposedly had a platonic relationship with."

THE DEATH OF A FRIEND

Three months prior to her disappearance, Jodi suffered the loss of a close friend named Billy Pruin. Pruin had just proposed to his girlfriend Gretchen Tusler and two days later he drove to Mason City to pick up a new tractor he had purchased. The next day, a friend went to his farmhouse and saw that his front door was ajar with the keys in the outside lock. He called out for his friend, received no answer, then he left.

No one had heard from Billy and then his mother went to his house to check on him. She would find him laying in a pool of blood, he had been shot in the chest.

Investigators listed his death as a suicide but later changed it to "undetermined".

His friends, Jodi included, could not believe that the jovial Billy committed suicide. He had just proposed to his girlfriend and bought a new tractor for a business. He had no reason to kill himself.

When Jodi disappeared, there was conjecture that the two deaths could be related.

His fiancee, Gretchen, was questioned after his death and stated that he often appeared "afraid of something" for weeks before his death.

Jodi voiced the same concerns prior to her disappearance. She written one of her best friends, Kelly Torgelson, revealing that "she was concerned for her safety, that she was being stalked."

Kelly would receive Jodi's letter in the mail on June 27th, 1995 at her home in Mississippi. The day that Jodi would be abducted.

"Jodi had reported that that a man in a pickup truck stopped and eyeballed her," Powell said. "This creeped her out. She felt as if someone was after her. So that is another theory that we have to go on in the case. Because of her position in the media and being a very attractive female, she was prone to have any nut ball start to fantasize and stalk her."

NO BODY, NO EVIDENCE

The investigators continued to grasp at straws while not pursuing anything against Vansice. They simply had nothing to pin him with.

Desperate for answers, the detectives and members of Jodi's family would meet with psychics in November of 1997.

"Psychics would be called upon a lot during the 1980s and 1990s," Powell said. "It was simply a sign of desperation from everyone involved. They needed anything, just anybody with some type of answer. So these charlatans would come in and they would go through the motions. When that happens, you know that the investigators have absolutely nothing."

Jodi's disappearance would leave her co-workers at KIMT devastated. Some left the business while others moved to other stations. Not one colleague that worked with Jodi during her tenure at KIMT remains with the station.

Wolfram, Jodi's friend and fellow broadcaster, would leave KIMT a few months after Jodi disappeared.

"They called me into the office and I thought they had found Jodi," Wolfram recalled. "Otherwise, why would all these people be in the office than to share that information. But there was talk on the internet

- chat rooms - he claimed he knew who had abducted Jodi. Gruesome details. Then the reason they had brought me in was the last communication was that Robin Wolfram would be next. From that point on - I had a police escort at night. From that point forward, I look at life differently. I think I used to look at life in rose colored glasses and everyone had a pure heart like Jodi. I realized evil exists right next door to good. It's like a veil. You reach your hand across to experience it. And it's not that easy."

NEW LEADS, MORE FALSE HOPES

Jodi's case would remain in the public eye and garnered renewed interest on the 20th year anniversary of her disappearance.

In a bizarre twist, photocopies of Jodi's personal diary were anonymously mailed to a local newspaper in June of 2008. The journal was eighty-four pages long and sent to the Mason City Globe Gazette. The diary had been placed in a large envelope with no return address. Days later, however, the sender had come forward.

It was the wife of the former Mason City Police Chief.

Her motive for sending the copy to the newspaper remains unclear.

JODI'S JOURNAL

Jodi would start "journaling" after she purchased Anthony Robbins Success program.

Her entries would reveal some of her personal thoughts and how she prioritized things in terms of work, family, and friends. Throughout the pages, she expressed her love for travel, socializing and her search for someone to share her life with.

"Remember," one of her first entries read, "there is no time better than now to begin practicing being the best I can be and living the way I want to live."

Jodi would continue to write about her goals and desire to get the "Huisentruit name out." She listed Paula Zahn and Kathy Gifford as her role models.

She wrote about her dating life briefly, talking about male friends and her love for dancing. She had met a man she liked during a cruise she had taken with her mother. "Why do I get hooked so fast?" she asked in one entry. "I'm lonely here at times and would like to have someone to share my life with. Sure I meet men — but none that really strikes me, or who follows thru."

"My No. 1 goal is to get a new job," she wrote in April 1995, two months before her disappearance.

"I'm recovering from Memorial Day Weekend, unbelievable — Indy 500 — a time of my life. Partied with so many wonderful people — Mario Andretti (world class racer), Joe Dumars (Detroit Pistons basketball player) and Tim Allen (TV star from 'Home Improvement'). Had an incredible weekend."

The latter part of her entries focused more on her activities as opposed to her goals.

"I stayed in Mason City this weekend to regroup, gather my thoughts and goals, read! And have Jodi time. I've enjoyed it. Church is very important to me as is putting myself and family ... at the top. I'm starting fresh at work this week — getting up at 3 a.m. — best newscast in the world — top 10 market — I really think I'll market myself for AZ. — see what they think about my accent. Or I'll move down there to produce."

Her final three entries all mention John Vansice.

"What a weekend, Surprise," Jodi wrote on June 11, 1995. "My Mason City/Clear Lake friends thru a big party for me! At a lounge, wild. It was in Clear Lake. They had a 16 gal keg – huge cake (with a skier) so much left. John Van Sice grilled 150 pork burgers, we were dancing on tables...dancing everywhere...Everyone had a ball. Video camera was rolling, cameras were clicking – oh what fun! Life is so good. The party made me feel so good."

"Last night John,...and I went to the Glen Miller Orchestra in Belmond," Jodi wrote on June 13th, 1995. "I have so many great viewers. People are so kind. This nice weather has me wild. I bought a new Mazda Miata, simply love it."

"Got home from a weekend road trip to Iowa City," Jodi wrote in her final entry. "oh we had fun! It was wild, partying and water skiing. We skied at the Coralville Res. I'm improving on the skis — hips up, lean, etc. John's son Trent gave me some great ski tip advice. Today, Sunday, it was raining in Mason City so didn't get any skiing in. I love it, it's addicting." Later on in the entry she wrote about her desire to move on from KIMT. "Great friends but professionally, I'm fed up. It's difficult finding a new job and I'm confused about agent and what to do."

The journals didn't reveal any clues that furthered the investigation. It remains a head-scratcher as to why the wife of the former police chief would forward the journal to the newspaper.

"The journals said a lot about Jodi's character," Powell said. "Reading through it is heartbreaking because you realize how much she loved her life, her family, and friends. She was on the road to self-improvement and listened to Tony Robbins' success tapes. She aspired to beyond what she was doing. She wanted to make her mark."

NEW SUSPECT

One new suspect that did emerge in recent years was serial rapist Tony Dejuan Jackson. Jackson was twenty-one years old at the time of Huisentruit's abduction and is now serving a life sentence in Minnesota for raping three women in 1997.

He was questioned about the crime and denied ever meeting Huisentruit or seeing her in public.

His former friend, however, stated otherwise.

Speaking anonymously, this friend would tell the Minneapolis news station KMSP that he had met Jackson because their girlfriends at the time were good friends. The source described an occasion where Jackson had invited him to get drinks where he knew Jodi was a regular.

The two then arrived at the South Bridge Lounge where they saw Jodi sitting at the bar.

He stated that Jackson walked right up to Jodi and began talking to her but he didn't hear the gist of their conversation.

Jackson was living in Mason City at the time and was attending North Iowa Community College. He hosted his own student talk show and wanted to pursue a career in broadcasting.

His friend thought that Jackson simply wanted to get career advice from Jodi not really thinking anything of their conversation until years later.

"My gut tells me that he probably did it," Jackson's friend said. "After all the stuff he's done since."

This suspicion of Jackson is corroborated with a neighbor who went out jogging early in the morning. She stated that the morning before she saw a young African American man, riding a bike outside the complex. He started biking ride beside her and she was spooked by him as it was so early in the morning.

Jackson would eventually be connected to over six sexual assaults on women from North Iowa to the St. Paul area in Minnesota.

He would arm himself with handcuffs, duct tape, mask and a gun as he stalked his victims. He threatened to kill his victims when they would not submit to him. One of his victims was eventually able to identify him as she worked with Jackson at a restaurant.

Jackson would write rap songs in prison that contained the lyric "stiffin' around Tiffin." Authorities believed that he may be referring to a silo in Tiffin, Iowa which he may have dumped her body. He had also told a cellmate that he was involved with a kidnapping of a news anchor.

Mason City police would not charge him, however, and it remains unclear why the eliminated him as a suspect.

As of this writing, John Vansice remains the primary person of interest. He has since moved to Phoenix, Arizona.

Jodi would be declared legally dead in May of 2001.

THE MURDER OF KARYN KUPCINET

OLIVIA WATSON

Chapter 1

In the latter half of 1963, Karyn Kupcinet was living in Hollywood while pursuing her one true dream: to become a famous starlet. She was constantly on the lookout for the role that would land her her big break. From an outsider's perspective, Kupcinet was well-equipped for and well on her way to stardom. Her life had all the ingredients: she had a wealthy, well-known father, an actor boyfriend whose career was gaining steam, and dark sultry looks that many would have died for. However, behind the scenes, not all was as it seemed.

In reality, Kupcinet's life was on a dramatic downward spiral in the latter half of 1963. Her relationship with her boyfriend, Andrew Prine, was strained at best and her mental health was deteriorating since undergoing an illegal abortion in July of that year. On November 28, 1963, she was dead.

Karyn Kupcinet's life began in a much-less dramatic manner than in which it was taken though. Karyn Kupcinet was born on March 6, 1941 in Chicago. As a young child, she acquired the nickname "Cookie." That was what her parents liked to call her, so was so sweet she'd give you a toothache.

Karyn did not get her sweet side from her mother though. Esther Kupcinet was often described as not caring about anyone unless they were famous. It was no surprise when she began grooming her young daughter to become an actress. She was from the Gold Coast in Chicago, a picturesque neighborhood that's home to Chicago's most affluent residents. Esther herself was a failed wannabe-dancer who imparted a love of the fame-filled lifestyle into her young daughter.

Her mother, Esther Kupcinet, would be the one to encourage Karyn to pursue acting as a career later in her life, but it would be her father who gave her the means to do so. Karyn's father was Irv Kupcinet, was a well-known and well-respected newspaper columnist for the *Chicago Sun-Times* who also worked as a television talk-show host and radio personality. To many in Chicago, he was known simply, but immediately, as "Kup."

Earlier in his life, Kupcinet was a Philadelphia Eagle. Kupcinet joined the NFL team after playing for the University of North Dakota. He was signed in 1935, and many thought he had a long career ahead of him playing for the team. Unfortunately, after playing only part of his first season, Kupcinet sustained a serious shoulder injury which benched him for the remainder of the season. After surgery Kupcinet was told that his shoulder would never fully recover, so Irv retired from his short run in the NFL.

After retiring from the NFL, Irv Kupcinet decided to combine his love and knowledge of sports with another passion of his that he developed in high school—reporting. Kupcinet took a job as a sports writer for the *Chicago Daily Times*. Kupcinet flourished at the job, and soon began writing about more than just sports. In 1948, Kupcinet was given his own column, *Kup's Column*, which chronicled the nightlife and celebrity scene of Chicago.

Kupcinet's success with the *Chicago Daily Times* filtered through many aspects of his career. The paper had built up his fame, and Kupcinet was now well-known in Chicago. In 1952, Kupcinet translated his fame for television when he landed his own talk show. Later, he was part of a group of talented talk show hosts who replaced Steve Allen on *The Tonight Show*.

By the time Kupcinet launched his talk show in 1952, he was almost a household name in Chicago. Thirty-four years and 15 Emmy Awards later, Kupcinet was a household name across America.

In 1957, Irv's daughter, Karyn Kupcinet, was in high school. She was 16 years old and starting to think about her future for the first time. She knew she wanted to be in the spotlight, she was a natural beauty and she admired her father's fame. Her mother suggested she pursue acting and Karyn loved the idea. She had participated in school plays since she was thirteen but had never thought of pursuing acting as a career before. Karyn soon discovered that having a father with his own television show syndicated on over 70 stations across America opened a lot of doors in Hollywood.

Chapter 2

During high school, Karyn Kupcinet decided she wanted to become a famous actress. She spent her senior year applying to arts colleges across the country and was accepted to Pine Manor College. After graduation, Kupcinet left her hometown and family for Boston, determined to hone her acting skills at the liberal arts college.

Kupcinet's time at Pine Manor was short-lived though. In fact, the young starlet-to-be studied in Boston for only a single semester before packing back up and moving to New York City. In New York, Kupcinet began studying at the Actors Studio, a membership organization for those who are determined to succeed in the world of show business.

Through connections she made at the Actors Studio, and through connections with producers she acquired through her father, Karyn landed her first professional role in the 1961 Jerry Lewis film *The Ladies Man*. In her first role, Kupcinet played a bit part as a young lady in a Hollywood boardinghouse alongside dozens of other young starlet wannabes.

Amongst the crowd of young ladies, Kupcinet managed to stand out. The same year, she appeared in two episodes of *Hawaiian Eye*, an episode of *The Andy Griffith Show*, and an episode of *The Donna Reed Show*.

Kupcinet was getting positive reviews for her roles, and went on to guest star in many other popular television shows. In 1962 she was awarded roles in *The Red Skeleton Show*, and *G.E. True*.

As well as these guest roles, Kupcinet also landed her first starring role in 1962 on the primetime series *Mrs. G. Goes to College*, which was later retitled *The Gertrude Berg Show* for its run. The premise of *The Gertrude Berg Show* was that a middle-aged Jewish widow enrolls in a college as a freshman after her children are all grown up. While at college, she interacts with a variety of younger students and her Cambridge University exchange professor, who was played by Cedric Hardwicke.

Kupcinet played the role of Carol, a classmate of Mrs. G. who dated her good friend Joe Caldwell, who was played by Skip Ward. Kupcinet's character had little dialogue, but her dark, sultry looks stood out from the background.

In 1962, Kupcinet also completed one of her first interviews as an actress on the rise. She was interviewed by the *Los Angeles Times* to help promote *Mrs. G. Goes to College*. This interview was supposed to promote her profile as a hirable, talented actress as well, but many instead thought it provided insight into the extreme pressure the young starlet was facing.

During the interview, Kupcinet spoke highly of her cast mates and the show, but had a difficult time talking about her own involvement in the program. When the questions turned to herself, Kupcinet talked exclusively about food and her body weight.

Despite facing an inner pressure, Kupcinet won more acting roles, which she was praised for. After *Mrs. G. Goes to College* finished its short run, Kupcinet appeared in *The Wide Country,* and *Going My Way*. While her role in these shows were short, her work on *The Wide Country* garnered the attention of one person in particular—the show's star Andrew Prine.

Andrew Prine was an actor who came to Hollywood from Florida in 1957 when he first appeared in a single episode of *U.S. Steel Hour*. By 1962, Prine had hit it big. In the same year, Prine was cast in both the Academy Award-nominated film, *The Miracle Worker*, as Helen Keller's older brother, and in the lead role of the NBC series *The Wide Country*.

The Wide Country was an American Western drama about two brothers who worked in the travelling rodeo circuit. The older brother Mitch, played by Earl Holliman, warns his brother about the dangers of following in his own footsteps in the bronco riding world, but Prine's character, Andy, refuses to listen.

In December of 1962, Andrew Prine crossed Karyn Kupcinet's path when she guest starred on *The Wide Country*. On screen, their characters never interacted, but off screen, the pair couldn't keep their eyes, or their hands, off one another.

The two rising stars began dating each other, and on paper they seemed to be a match made in heaven. They were both young, attractive, and chasing stardom. In reality, however, the relationship was very strained.

Once the puppy love phase of their relationship passed, Prine was hesitant to make the relationship exclusive. They were both busy workers with packed schedules and they were young. Prine had just begun to make his mark in Hollywood, and didn't want to settle down or dedicate too much of his time to another person. Most of all, though, Prine was worried that Kupcinet would be a mar on his good reputation.

Although she was receiving good review for her work, Kupcinet was beginning to crumble under the enormous pressure she felt to follow in her father's footsteps of success. Kupcinet began abusing diet pills in 1961. Diet pills in the 1960s were not the same as they are today. Little was known about the properties of many ingredients, so the FDA often approved substances that were not safe for consumption.

One of the most popular diet pills at the time was Obetrol, which was approved by the FDA on January 19, 1960. Obetrol was marketed as a way to lose and control a person's weight. It was a popular drug at the time, and many believed that it was effective in helping them feel more energetic and lose weight quicker, which is not surprising as it was a formulation of three amphetamine mixed salts, including methamphetamine.

Along with her addiction to diet pills, Kupcinet also began abusing prescription drugs in the early 1960s. This combination proved too much for Kupcinet, who began to deteriorate. Despite coming from a wealthy family who were happy to support the young star, Kupcinet began shoplifting from popular stores and was arrested in 1963 for stealing two books, a sweater, and a pair of capris pants. Andrew Prine was mortified by Kupcinet's arrest, worried about how it would reflect on him through their connection.

By August of 1963, Karyn Kupcinet's relationship with Andrew Prine was all but over. In the previous month, Kupcinet underwent an illegal abortion in Tijuana after becoming pregnant with Prine's child. Prine had encouraged Kupcinet to undergo the procedure to protect both of their reputations and because he had no intention of marrying Kupcinet as she had hoped.

After the procedure, Prine declared their relationship over and began dating other women, but Kupcinet wasn't about to let her first love end quite yet.

Chapter 3

By the latter half of 1963, Karyn Kupcinet had lost her touch on reality. Her first love, Andrew Prine, had finally severed all ties to the young starlet due to her addiction to prescription and diet pills, but she wasn't ready to let go. Kupcinet began stalking Prine at his home, and would write about these experiences in her diary.

July 30th read, *Andy with Anna. Me watched from hedge. Awful. Nightmares.*

August 20th followed, *So humiliated by Andy's lack of interest.*

On October 29th she wrote, *Andy acting ugly. Complete indifference. Scene at his house. I'm hysterical.*

While these short messages tell a foreboding tale, the worst entries came from November.

On the 4th, after hiding in Prine's attic, she wrote *Wish I were dead*, and 24 days later on November 28, 1963, she was.

Months before her death, though, Kupcinet put a great deal of effort into making her Prine believe that her life, and his, were in great danger.

Along with stalking Prine and his new girlfriends at his house, Kupcinet began sending letters to Prine. But these were no ordinary letters. Kupcinet would put together threatening and profanity-filled hate mail composed of words cut from magazines. She sent these letters anonymously to Prine, sometimes skipping the post and dropping them off right on his doorstep.

But Prine suspected Kupcinet was behind these letters, so he confronted her. Luckily for her, Kupcinet had thought ahead and composed several similar letters to herself, claiming they had also been anonymously sent to her. She was hoping this would inspire a desire to protect in Prine, but he remained wary of his unstable ex.

Prine always remembered these startling letters. After Kupcinet's death, he had police examine the letters to see if they could determine who had sent them. The answer was no surprise to him. Investigators were able to find Kupcinet's fingerprints all over them, including on the sticky side of the scotch tape used to secure the frightening messages to the paper.

On the night of November 28, 1963, Kupcinet had dinner with her close friends Mark Goddard and his wife Marcia Rogers Goddard at their Beverly Hills House. She was an hour late for dinner, arriving at 7:30p.m. when the dinner had begun at 6:30p.m. The Goddard's later told police that Kupcinet was surprised they had waited for her to eat, and she hardly touched her food throughout the meal.

This was normal for Kupcinet though, who had struggled with body issues and the pressure to stay thin since high school. What wasn't normal, however, was the state Kupcinet was in. Marcia Goddard told authorities that that night Kupcinet acted very strangely during their last meal together. Her lips seemed numb and her voice sounded funny. She moved her head at odd angles and her pupils were incredibly small.

Mark Goddard had confronted Kupcinet about this odd behaviour during the meal, accusing her of being high. Kupcinet immediately began to cry and deny being on any substances and instead blamed her behaviour on the unsubstantiated claim that she had found an abandoned baby on her doorstep earlier that day.

An hour after she arrived, Kupcinet left the Goddard's house in a taxi cab headed home. She promised to call her friends the next day when she was feeling better. After arriving home, she was visited by two friends of hers, Edward Rubin and Robert Hathaway, who also happened to be neighbors and close friends with her ex-boyfriend.

According to Hathaway and Rubin, the three friends watched TV and had coffee with Kupcinet before she fell asleep beside them on the couch. They woke her up and helped her get to her bedroom. After this, the men said they turned the TV off, locked the doors, and left around 11:15p.m.

The men then headed over to Robert Hathaway's house where they were joined by Andrew Prine himself. The three friends chatted and watched TV until 3:00a.m.

The next day, the Goddard's waited for Karyn Kupcinet's call, but it never came. They figured she must have either forgotten or was too embarrassed about her behaviour to check in so they waited a couple of days. They hardly went half a week without hearing from the young woman, so they figured she would call soon enough.

On the third day with no call, the Goddard's began to panic, so they decided to visit Kupcinet's West Hollywood apartment to make sure she was okay. What they found shocked them both, and would forever remain in their memories.

Chapter 4

November 30, 1963. West Hollywood. It's been three days since Mark and Marcia sent Karyn Kupcinet home from their dinner party after her strange behaviour. That night, Kupcinet had promised to call the couple the next morning to check in, but she never did. Mark now feared that his good friend had died from a drug overdose.

The couple arrived at Kupcinet's West Hollywood apartment around noon. They walked through the unlocked front door and found a horrific sight—Karyn Kupcinet was lying face-down on the couch. She was completely nude.

The Goddard's immediately contacted the police, who began investigating immediately. Initially, it looked like the Goddard's suspicions had been true, that Kupcinet had overdosed on the number of drugs she had been abusing over the course of the last few years. Investigators found prescriptions and numerous bottles of Desoxyn, Miltown, Amvicel, Thyroid extract and Modaline strewn around Kupcinet's bathroom.

There was other evidence in the apartment that Kupcinet may have taken her own life; the strongest piece of evidence they found to support this was a cryptic note found in her bedroom which reflected her emotions regarding her life, her parents, her self-image, and her boyfriend.

This note was written in a haphazard fashion, a similar style to her diary entries. One of the most poignant pieces of the note read:

I'm no good. I'm not really that pretty. My figure's fat and will never be the way my mother wants it. Why must I be so alone. What's the use of living with nothing to believe it?

Clearly, Kupcinet was not in a good mental state in the months leading up to her death, and this note proved that without a doubt.

Also at the scene, investigators realized that Kupcinet had not died that day. In fact, she had been dead for several days. Her body had begun decomposing and there was evidence that flies had found Kupcinet first, laying eggs in her scalp. None of the eggs had hatched yet.

Additionally, there was some evidence of distress around Kupcinet's living room. The TV was on, but the volume was turned almost all the way down. Nearby the couch was a metal coffee pot and a brandy glass full of cigarette butts that had been overturned on the floor. A coffee cup sat on a side table across a room next to a pile of matches that had been shredded and cut up by scissors.

In Kupcinet's bedroom, investigators found that all of her dresser drawers were opened and most of the contents had been flung across the room.

Because it was clear that Kupcinet's mental health was unstable leading up to her death, police weren't sure if the mess they found in the apartment was a sign that a struggle had occurred or simply another indication of Kupcinet's mental distress. Form the scene alone, they were unable to determine whether Kupcinet had died from an attack, an accident, or an unintentional suicide.

Kupcinet's body was transferred to a nearby coroner. Sidney Korshak, a Los Angeles based lawyer that had been friends with the Kupcinet family for years, officially identified her body the next day. Shortly after Kupcinet was officially identified, an autopsy was performed on her corpse. The results of which shocked everyone in the case.

After the coroner completed the autopsy, it was determined that Karyn Kupcinet had in fact been murdered. According to the coroner, she had been dead for two days, and her cause of death was manual strangulation due to injuries on her neck that included a compression fracture to the left side of her hyoid bone with deep soft tissue hemorrhages in her neck, thyroid gland, and larynx.

After the autopsy, Kupcinet's body was returned to her hometown, Chicago, where she was laid to rest just outside of the city in Skokie, Illinois. While over 500 people attended her funeral, Andrew Prine did not.

After Karyn was laid to rest, the Kupcinet family was ready for investigators to discover who had murdered their beloved daughter so they could begin to heal. They had no idea at the time the media frenzy that would surround their daughter's murder later, or that the mystery of her death would never be officially solved.

Chapter 5

Karyn Kupcinet's death was initially highly publicized in the Los Angeles media, especially when it was discovered that another up-and-coming star was the main suspect—Andrew Prine. The LAPD believed that Prine was one of the only people who would have had a motive to kill Kupcinet. If she died, he would no longer be haunted by his ex-girlfriend who refused to let him forget her. As well, Prine strongly suspected that Kupcinet had been behind the threatening letters that tormented him.

As well, Prine had spoken to Kupcinet over the phone several times the day before she died, arguing, which was overheard by multiple sources. Prine had an airtight alibi for the night that Kupcinet was killed, but his friends, Robert Hathaway and Edward Rubin, had admitted to spending time with Kupcinet the night she was killed. The pair had told police that they left Kupcinet's apartment that night around 11:30p.m., but the only witness who could corroborate this was Andrew Prine himself.

Unfortunately, Prine, Hathaway, and Rubin had all admitted to being in Kupcinet's apartment shortly before her death, police were forced to accredit all physical evidence of them in the apartment to other times. They found no physical evidence that could directly tie either of the three men to Kupcinet at the time of her death.

The LAPD, along with Kupcinet's family, was pretty sure the three men were responsible for Karyn's death, but pretty sure doesn't stand up in a court of law. None of the men ever faced charges in the crime.

With no exciting breaks in the case, Karyn Kupcinet's murder quickly fell out of the newspapers in Los Angeles and out of the minds of its residents. It wasn't until 1967 that Kupcinet's story was thought of by many outside of her own family.

In 1967, Penn Jones Jr., a researcher with a love of conspiracy theories, self-published the book *Forgive My Grief II*, which attempted to present a set of facts as evidence that the JFK assassination hadn't happened the way the media and the government had claimed.

John F. Kennedy was assassinated the day before Kupcinet died. According to Jones, who cited an Associated Press story, an unidentified woman had called her local operator twenty minutes before the assassination of the President, warning of the impending attack. Jones believed that the unidentified woman was Karyn Kupcinet.

Jones cited as proof the fact that the call had come from California, and that Kupcinet's murder could have been connected to her spilling a deadly secret. Karyn, Jones claimed, heard about the assassination from her father, Irv Kupcinet, who allegedly had been told by Jack Ruby, Oswald's killer, whom Irv had met in the 1940s.

Irv Kupcinet continued to deny that he or his daughter had any knowledge of the President's assassination before the rest of America right up until his own death in 2003. Kupcinet wrote about his daughter in *Kup's Column*. In 1992, NBC's *Today Show* ran a segment on mysterious deaths that occurred after JFK's assassination, including Karyn's death. Irv again spoke out against the idea that Karyn had any role in the story surrounding the assassination. He insisted again that both his family and the LAPD knew exactly who had been responsible for her death—Andrew Prine, Robert Hathaway, and Edward Rubin—there just wasn't, nor would there ever be, enough evidence to prove it to a court.

When Irv Kupcinet passed away on November 10, 2003, He was laid to rest next to his daughter and wife, who passed away in 2001. Irv's death marked the end of an era to many Chicagoans, just as it put an end to the investigation into Karyn Kupcinet's death.

In her quest to be seen on every silver screen, Karyn Kupcinet lost sight of herself. Striving to be skinny, the young starlet abused her mind and body excess amounts of prescription and diet pills. When her mind went, so did her chances of finding love and happiness, no matter how hard she tried to maintain it.

Karyn Kupcinet's final appearance on television came a year after her death in 1964. Kupcinet had guest starred on an episode of *Perry Mason*, which had been in post-production at the time of her death and the following year. To many who saw her performance, it seemed the young beauty was just beginning her rise to fame, but she was already gone, taken from the world many years too early.